CHILDREN'S
MINISTRY
VOLUNTEER HANDBOOK

CHILDREN'S MINISTRY
VOLUNTEER HANDBOOK

Equipping You to Serve

First Edition: Year 2019
Children's Ministry Volunteer Handbook / Outreach, Inc.
Paperback ISBN: 978-1-946453-75-4
eBook ISBN: 978-1-946453-76-1

CHURCHLEADERS
PRESS

Colorado Springs

CONTENTS

CHILDREN'S MINISTRY
VOLUNTEER HANDBOOK

Equipping You to Serve

Written by
Danielle Bell
Heather Dunn
Brooke Gibson
Dale Hudson
Kal Otis
Katie Wetherbee

General Editor
Stephanie J. Martin

CHURCHLEADERS
PRESS

Colorado Springs

Gibson, Dale Hudson, Kal Otis, and Katie Wetherbee. Each of these seasoned children's ministry leaders has devoted years to loving kids in Jesus' name and leading volunteers to do the same.

Whether you're new to children's ministry or have been serving for a while, you'll find the help you need to turn any mess you encounter into a ministry that changes children's lives—and yours! You'll find age-appropriate tips that might even keep you from getting slapped. (Just kidding!) You'll discover answers to the questions and challenges you may face along the way.

In Matthew 18:1, Jesus' disciples ask him, "Who, then, is the greatest in the kingdom of heaven?" Jesus invites a little child to stand among them and then reveals his love for children: "Truly I tell you, unless you change and become like little children, you will never enter the kingdom of heaven. Therefore, whoever takes the lowly position of this child is the greatest in the kingdom of heaven. And whoever welcomes one such child in my name welcomes me" (verses 3-5).

When you serve children in Jesus' name, you're dealing with greatness in God's kingdom. God bless you in this very important ministry to children in Jesus' name!

— **Christine Yount Jones,**
Content Director at *Outreach*

INTRODUCTION
to the *Outreach Ministry Guides* Series

*Each of you should use whatever gift you have received to serve others, as
faithful stewards of God's grace in its various forms*
(1 Peter 4:10).

his handbook is part of a series designed to equip and
empower church volunteers for effective ministry. If you're
reading this, chances are you're a church volunteer. Thanks for
your willingness to serve!

Several things make this handbook unique:

- The content is specific and practical for your given
  area of ministry.
- The information is compiled by experienced
  ministry practitioners—folks who've worked, served,
  and helped to train others in this particular area.
- It's written with you—a ministry volunteer—in
  mind.

Within these pages, you'll find three sections. The first
gives a brief overview of fundamental principles to provide you
with a solid foundation for the ministry area in which you're
serving.

Section 2 unpacks various roles and responsibilities.
Understanding your role and the roles of your fellow teammates
helps the ministry team serve together well.

Finally, Section 3 provides a multitude of practical ministry tools. These ideas and tips will help you demonstrate Jesus' love to the people you serve at your church.

Whether you're a first-time volunteer or a seasoned veteran, my prayer is that the information and practical tools in this handbook will encourage and assist you. May God bless and guide you in your ministry!

— **Matt Lockhart,** Project Manager

INTRODUCTION

to the *Children's Ministry Volunteer Handbook*

"*I*n the race to a child's heart, the first one there wins." That quote from researcher George Barna sums up why children's ministry is one of the most vital programs in the local church.

> "If I could relive my life, I would devote my entire ministry to reaching children for God."

Studies repeatedly show that most people become Christians before age 18. That puts children's ministry volunteers at the epicenter of exciting conversations and choices that have eternal impact. Perhaps that's why nineteenth-century evangelist D.L. Moody said, "If I could relive my life, I would devote my entire ministry to reaching children for God."

Because children's ministry changes lives, it's one of the most rewarding ways to get involved at church. And as you'll soon discover, it's also a lot of fun! This handbook provides an overview of children's ministry, including a bit of history and theory. But most of the content consists of practical advice and ideas from in-the-field experts. You'll be able to implement many of these tips right away, no matter your experience level.

To learn more about the impact you'll have as a children's ministry volunteer, read the short chapters in Section 1. For developmental insights about specific age groups and classroom management techniques geared toward those groups, dive into Section 2. The final section covers a wide range of relevant ministry topics, with answers about everything from learning styles to safety procedures. Be sure to check out the helpful FAQs and resource lists, as well as Discussion Questions that will spark interesting conversations among your ministry teammates.

Make the most of this handbook by first zeroing in on the chapters that address your interests or immediate questions. As time allows, review the other parts to learn about other ministry areas and age groups. Jot down notes, questions, and ideas along the way.

Blessings as you begin this exciting volunteer adventure!

— **Stephanie J. Martin,** General Editor

SECTION 1

THE HEART OF
CHILDREN'S MINISTRY

FOREWORD

$\mathcal{J}$ remember the first children's ministry class I taught one fateful summer, in a small country church in Oklahoma. Because I was a brand-new Christian with lots of passion for serving God, I came home after my sophomore year of college to do whatever my little church needed.

Turns out, they needed someone to lead the kids. The children's ages ranged from 3 to 17, and we all met together. It's what experts now call a mixed-age group—and was it ever mixed! Girls and boys of all ages clamored for my attention.

"They keep sitting so close to me!" I told my mom, who wisely advised me to just put my arm around their shoulders. They snuggled even closer. One day, after calling my name repeatedly in the large group, a frustrated preteen turned me around and slapped me across the cheek. And an elderly helper accidentally drank the bleach from the object lesson, even though I'd placed the liquid on a high shelf.

I was a mess! The class was a mess!

But in the middle of all that chaos, we were making a difference in children's lives. They had a safe place to come learn with people who loved them. They had something fun to do on Wednesday nights that kept them—at least the older ones—out of trouble. That summer, many kids got to know Jesus as their Savior.

The mess became a ministry.

What I would've given that summer for a handbook like this! I needed the practical tips and insightful advice from children's ministry experts such as Danielle Bell, Heather Dunn, Brooke

CHAPTER 1

CHILDREN'S MINISTRY 101

*I*n the late 1700s, Christian outreach to young people began in England—and then the United States—as a way to help poor children who worked in factories and textile mills. On Sundays, their only day off, these kids (often orphans) tended to go hungry and turned to crime. So people began offering classes, along with food and warm clothes, for kids on that day of the week, when they had no other place to go. Teachers provided basic instruction in reading, writing, and morality, using the Bible as the "textbook."

Various religious groups soon followed that model, making Sunday school a common childhood experience during the 1800s. As America's public education system was established, "church school" narrowed its focus to spiritual practices such as prayer, Christian hymns, catechism, and Scripture memorization. In its early forms, Sunday school was the primary tool for church growth and evangelism, while today it focuses more on spiritual growth and discipleship.

Sunday school, which serves all those purposes well, now fits under the wider umbrella of children's ministry, sometimes referred to as "kidmin." That often includes traditional Sunday morning classes plus small groups, children's choir, midweek worship, children's church, and programs such as vacation Bible school. Volunteers from teens to senior citizens—and sometimes paid staff—dedicate time and energy to nurturing children's faith in meaningful and memorable ways. Your help furthers not only the work of your church but also of God's kingdom.

In churches of all sizes, children's ministry is valued and vital. Scripture addresses the importance of ministering to all people, as well as to children specifically. In Deuteronomy, an Old Testament book filled with instructions for life, God makes it clear that parents should teach their children his Word and everything he's done for them (for example, see Deuteronomy 4:9-10; 6:4-8, 20-25; 11:18-21). Psalm 78 is a plea for the Israelites, God's chosen people, to share their history—and God's faithfulness throughout it—with their descendants. Verse 4 says, "We will tell the next generation the praiseworthy deeds of the Lord, his power, and the wonders he has done." That, in a nutshell, is the purpose and heart of children's ministry: telling future generations about Jesus.

Three of the four Gospels recount Jesus calling children to him and saying the kingdom of God belongs to them. When parents approach Jesus seeking a blessing for their children, his disciples try to send them away. But Jesus says, "Let the little children come to me, and do not hinder them, for the kingdom of heaven belongs to such as these" (Matthew 19:14).

Accounts of Jesus interacting with children show that he not only loves and warmly welcomes them but also believes they're more than capable of having faith. In fact, Jesus says a childlike faith is the purest type—and the type of faith all his followers should strive for (Matthew 18:3). From babies to preteens, all children are important to Jesus. Even if older students start to bristle at being called "children," they always remain children of God.

When Jesus' disciples argue about who among them is the greatest, Jesus calls a child over and says, "Whoever takes the lowly position of this child is the greatest in the kingdom of heaven" (Matthew 18:4). He also promises, "Whoever welcomes one of these little children in my name welcomes me; and whoever welcomes me does not welcome me but the one who sent me" (Mark 9:37). When children step foot in your classroom, choir room, or any other area where you might meet, you have the privilege of welcoming Jesus, as well as God the Father. In other words, you're serving children, the church, and the Lord!

Today, ministry to children is as important as ever. Research consistently shows the importance of early exposure to matters of faith. A Barna Group study found that 43 percent of all people who become Christians do so before age 13, and 64 percent do so before age 18. That information, summarized in the Barna report "Evangelism Is Most Effective Among Kids," provides parents and teachers with a "primary window of opportunity for effectively reaching people with the good news of Jesus' death and resurrection," note Barna researchers. That's when people "develop their frames of reference for the remainder of their life—especially theologically and morally." To develop spiritually, the study adds, kids need adults in their lives who consistently explain and model biblical truth.

> Kids need adults in their lives who consistently explain and model biblical truth.

Outreach to children also is a major conduit for welcoming new families and helping them get involved and invested in church life. In the process, your congregation grows and becomes more vibrant. A *Children's Ministry Magazine* survey finds that families with kids tend to be "some of the most active and committed" church members. According to survey results, summarized in the article "Children's Ministry's Impact on Your Church," 65 percent of parents indicate they're regularly involved with the children's ministry. And 62 percent say children's ministry is a key factor in whether they'll stay involved with their current congregation.

The benefits of children's ministry extend well beyond the church and classroom. The majority of parents say these programs positively impact their children as well as their entire family. When *Children's Ministry Magazine* asked parents to rank the benefits of their church's ministry to kids, the top answer was "It helps my kids develop a personal, growing faith." Sixty percent of parents said the children's ministry at their church "has impacted them moderately or somewhat," and that they've used the materials their kids bring home from Sunday school. In other words, the time and love you devote as a volunteer has profound ripple effects.

> The time and love you devote as a volunteer has profound ripple effects.

As impressive as statistics may be, what matters most is that children's ministry impacts individual hearts and minds. By teaching kids about Jesus and his love for them, you plant spiritual seeds that last for a lifetime—and throughout eternity. From a young age, children can learn to listen to, appreciate, and follow what the Bible says. They'll turn to you with questions, observe your actions and attitudes, and find joy in sharing their developing faith with others. Children's ministry provides a solid foundation on which young people's faith can grow, while offering age-appropriate tools for being in relationship with God and others.

Children's programs draw families to church and encourage them to discover more about faith together. Ministry to little ones provides families with an entry to faith, a place to celebrate spiritual milestones, and many avenues to discover and use their God-given talents. Countless church leaders credit Sunday school teachers for sparking their love for Jesus and his Word. What an exciting journey you're beginning as a children's ministry volunteer!

Working with children in this capacity is a big responsibility, but don't be intimidated by the task ahead. The good news is that you're not alone, and the results don't depend on your effort or creativity. As Philippians 2:13 says, "For it is God who works in you to will and to act in order to fulfill his good purpose."

CHAPTER 2

ANATOMY OF A CHILDREN'S MINISTRY

*A*s with churches, children's ministries come in many shapes and sizes. There's no one most effective way to teach kids about Jesus and his love. The best approach to children's ministry for your church is the way that fits your church the best. The director, staff, and volunteers likely will need to experiment a bit, making changes when circumstances and conditions warrant. Certain aspects of the program may be "tried and true," rarely varying from year to year, while others contain more wiggle room for trying something new. Change can be fun for children as well as adults, but it's important not to mess with success merely for the sake of tinkering.

In very small congregations, children of all ages may be grouped together for Sunday school. As churches grow in size, they often add a nursery and preschool component, as well as elementary classes. Younger children tend to prefer predictability, so it's best to keep them in the same area or room for the entire class period. Variation and movement tend to be easier with older children, so learning activities can extend to different spaces—as long as kids stay with the same people and know what to expect.

Various options exist for Sunday-morning classes, midweek programming, and special events:

- Traditional Sunday school is modeled after "regular" school, with children divided by ages or grade levels. For the most part, kids learn in classrooms, with lessons tailored specifically to each level. Strong relationships develop between children and leaders as they spend time learning and growing together.

- Another format that's become popular is called "large group/small group." First, children all gather in a large group to worship together and learn a Bible lesson. Then they split into smaller groups, led by older youth or adults, to dig deeper into the lesson. (Depending on numbers, kids may or may not be grouped according to age.) This format allows speakers, teachers, and musicians to lead from their individual strengths during large groups. Strong relationships are then built during small groups.

- A "rotations" format allows adults to teach in their preferred method, while exposing children to the most variety. One person may specialize in arts and crafts, for example, while another is skilled at drama and another at storytelling. Each leader stays in a certain place while groups of children, each led by a volunteer, rotate through the different areas. Several rotations may occur during a single class session, or children may rotate to various areas weekly or monthly. Benefits of this format include increased creativity and the time to explore one topic from multiple perspectives.

- Multigenerational formats offer learning opportunities in family-friendly settings. Some churches offer one combined worship service for all ages, from adults to infants. Sometimes children are excused partway through to attend children's church or an abbreviated class. Some churches offer a separate "family service," giving worshipers devotions or talking points to use at home throughout the week.

For each of these models, many curriculum options are available. Most follow a "scope and sequence," meaning there's a plan to give children a solid biblical foundation during their years in the ministry. Publishers usually post a curriculum's scope and sequence online for easy access by volunteers and parents.

Churches that belong to a larger Christian denomination or faith body may use the materials produced by that group's publishing arm. Some churches write their own curriculum but still have a long-term plan for covering the entire Bible and basics of the Christian faith. No matter the source of your lesson materials, take time to know the plan for your class. That provides long-term perspective for what you'll cover during your teaching tenure. It also helps you share with parents what children will be learning during the upcoming weeks and months.

> No matter the source of your lesson materials, take time to know the plan for your class.

Typically, lesson plans walk through the Bible in two to three years, following a systematic journey from Genesis through Revelation. Some plans alternate quarters (typically 13-week chunks) between Old and New Testament lessons. Others use a thematic approach, such as characteristics of God or the fruit of the Spirit.

Near Christmas and Easter, the two most important Christian holidays, regular lesson plans may be set aside briefly to focus specifically on Jesus' birth, death, and resurrection. During the summer, some children's ministry programs maintain a regular Sunday school schedule, some take a brief break, and others try something new. From June through August, for example, an all-ages group of children might meet to explore a "stand-alone" topic, such as the Ten Commandments or the parables of Jesus.

These days, most curriculum comes ready to use, requiring minimal preparation by volunteers. Lessons usually include scripts of everything a teacher needs to say, as well as step-by-step directions for crafts and games. Depending on your director's guidance and your comfort level with ad-libbing, you can adhere to scripts closely or loosely. The internet is a great source of additional craft and game ideas on a wide range of Bible topics. Keep a few extra ideas handy, in case you have time to fill after a lesson.

Family-based take-home materials are another helpful curriculum component. These handouts recap the day's lesson and key points, list Bible verses (possibly to memorize), and offer extension opportunities or devotions so parents can lead spiritual growth at home during the week. The children's ministry director or administrative assistant also may produce a newsletter to keep families informed about lesson topics, class schedules, and church happenings.

CHAPTER 3

SPACE AND PLACE

*B*ehind-the-scenes logistics such as classroom space and storage might not be your responsibility as a volunteer, but make sure you know where various ages meet and where supplies are located. If you don't understand why items are in certain places or organized in certain ways, be sure to ask. Understanding the reasons can help you be more effective and efficient.

Your "in-the-field" interactions with children and parents may inspire ideas for improvement. If you notice something, speak up! Your suggestions can benefit you, your teammates, and your students.

Children's ministry volunteers tend to become experts at winging it--making do with whatever happens to be available at a given time. Prepare to be flexible, especially when you're starting out. As you get more familiar with your role, you'll adapt and find innovative ways to make things work. You'll also grow more comfortable requesting what you need in order to be successful. Also remember that you can usually adapt lesson plans based on the available time, resources, and supplies. Ask the director for guidance with this, as needed.

> You can usually adapt lesson plans based on the available time, resources, and supplies.

Some churches and children's ministries rent space in schools or storefronts, which can make "space and place" decisions more complicated. If there's one larger room, maybe you can creatively transform it into several smaller areas. If there's an assortment of smaller spaces, determine which age groups—and how many children—fit best in each.

In case you need to make your classroom totally portable, wheels are your best friend. Invest in a cabinet on wheels from a store such as IKEA and request a place to keep it. Put everything you use each week into bins in the cabinet, keeping extra supplies at home. If a cabinet won't work, try a suitcase or craft tote with wheels.

Churches that have the luxury of their own regular spaces for children's ministry likely follow daycare and school regulations. General room-capacity guidelines range from eight to 12 children in nursery and toddler rooms, to 20 in elementary classrooms. Recommended volunteer-to-child ratios range from 1-to-2 in the nursery to 1-to-8 in elementary classrooms. However, at least two unrelated adults should always be in every room, regardless of how many children are present. If only two babies are in the nursery, for example, two volunteers are still needed.

Safety and security always must be at the forefront, as chapter 15 discusses in more detail. "Space and place," involves knowing where bathrooms and emergency exits are located, being aware of any stairs to navigate, and assessing how many children one adult can safely supervise—and carry, if needed—in case of emergency. Chapter 16 addresses emergencies more comprehensively.

In general, it's best to keep youngest children on the main floor, with a direct emergency exit. Nursery and toddler rooms should have an evacuation crib with extra-large wheels for easy transport. Preschool rooms should have a wide rope with knots tied in it for children to use whenever they move from one room to another (even to the bathroom). This helps them learn to walk in a line and to use the rope during an emergency situation without alarm.

Also consider ease of access and movement for children as well as families. Hallway width, for example, is often an overlooked space issue. Parents tend to bunch up while they're waiting to drop off or pick up children, so hallways should be at least 8 feet wide.

For more age-specific tips about classroom space, see the chapters in Section 2.

CHAPTER 4

A PHILOSOPHY OF MINISTRY

*W*hat is your children's ministry all about? What are its values and how are they expressed? That, in a nutshell, is a ministry philosophy. Terms commonly used to describe this philosophy include *mission, vision, goals,* and *guiding principles.* Sometimes they're used interchangeably or in combination. The important thing is that thought goes into the program and all its components.

A ministry's mission generally matches that of the larger congregation—and perhaps even of the Christian church worldwide. Followers of Jesus are involved with ministry to praise and spread his name through worship, education, fellowship, service, and outreach. Examples of mission-related terminology include "Love God, love others" and "Reach the world with the life-changing news of Jesus Christ." Although mission can be expressed in various ways, make sure the mission of your church—and its children's ministry—reflects Jesus. Learn and embrace that mission so you can share it with others.

The vision typically involves the practical pathway or the "how." How will you reach the world, your neighborhood, or the children in your care? Some churches answer that primarily through worship, while others focus on evangelism. Different congregations may specialize in small groups, music ministry, dynamic preaching and teaching, planting other churches, or a vibrant youth or children's ministry. All of these are great, if they're what God calls a particular group of people to do. Vision sets various churches and ministries apart from one another. God needs and uses all types of churches, just as he loves and uses all types of people.

For a Christ-centered children's ministry, the main goal is always to share the good news of Jesus. Only when you know where you're heading can you start planning and preparing program specifics. That end goal becomes a filter for every single thing you do.

To have a true Christ-centered ministry, the curriculum, weekly lessons, activities, programs, and events should continually point to Jesus. Everyone involved with the ministry should regularly step back to evaluate whether they're staying on track to reach the main goal. Reflect as a team and individually, asking: When kids leave this program, what will they ultimately take with them?

> When kids leave this program, what will they ultimately take with them?

Beyond that ultimate goal, churches and ministries usually set other goals aimed at quantifying their vision—and whether it's being accomplished. In a children's ministry, measurable goals may include attendance, faith commitments, Scripture memory, parental involvement, service hours, or progress through a defined set of spiritual milestones. Check with the director about your program's specific goals. Accomplishing them requires a team effort and dedication, but both the process and the end results are incredibly rewarding.

Guiding principles are the biblical foundations on which all the actions and practices of a church or ministry are based. These tend to line up quite closely with the vision. Ask the children's ministry director or pastor about guiding principles. Make sure those are clear, and then embrace them as you plan and teach lessons, interact with kids and parents, and partner with other staff and volunteers.

These examples of guiding principles for children's ministry are followed by the Scripture passages on which they're based:

- The Bible, as God's holy and perfect Word, has complete authority over our beliefs and actions (Isaiah 55:11; Romans 15:4; 1 Thessalonians 2:13; 2 Timothy 3:16-17).

- God loves us so much that he sent Jesus, his Son, to die for us. Salvation and eternal life in heaven are found only through Jesus (John 3:16-17; 14:6).

- All people are sinners in need of God's grace, which he offers freely through Jesus' death and resurrection (Romans 3:23-24; Ephesians 2:8-9).

- God the Holy Spirit lives in our hearts to strengthen our faith as we follow Jesus (John 14:26; Romans 8:11).

- Children are important to God, and he loves them deeply, as his chosen creations (Psalm 139:13-16; Matthew 19:14; Mark 9:35-37).

- Primary responsibility for Christian training belongs to a child's parents and family members (Deuteronomy 4:9-10; 6:4-8, 20-25; 11:18-21).

- We're all members of one body, of which Christ is the head (1 Corinthians 12:14-27; Romans 12:4-8).

- God has a plan and a purpose for everyone (Jeremiah 29:11; Philippians 2:12-13).

- Christians glorify God by reflecting the image of his Son, Jesus (Exodus 9:16; Isaiah 43:5-7; Romans 8:28-30; 15:5-6; 1 John 2:3-6).

- God, our Servant-King, calls us to humbly serve him and other people, just as he serves us (John 13:14-15; Philippians 2:1-8; Colossians 3:17).

From a practical standpoint, a ministry's philosophy shines through in day-to-day best practices that all staff members and volunteers follow. These include:

- Every lesson is Bible-based, reveals important information about Jesus and his love, inspires awe and worship, and emphasizes that we're all part of God's grand story, which continues to unfold.
- The program values, includes, and cares for all children and families, ministering to them through word and deed.
- The ministry has a long-term plan for the spiritual growth of all children (curriculum scope and sequence, ages and stages of spiritual growth, celebrations for faith milestones).
- The ministry has a clear—and clearly communicated—philosophy and structure (mission, vision, and guiding principles; how kids are grouped and taught; plans for growth).
- Children experience a variety of age-appropriate ways to grow in and practice their faith. Examples include worship, singing, Bible reading, prayer, art, drama, role-playing, object lessons, crafts, and games. Leaders also take into account various learning styles and methods.
- Children and volunteers look forward to classes and events because they're engaging, meaningful, and memorable.
- Children are encouraged to grow in their relationship with Jesus and to make their own personal faith commitments.
- Staff and volunteers focus on Jesus and sharing his love, remembering that they serve as important role models for children and parents.

- Staff and volunteers pray for one another and for the children in their care.
- Volunteers thrive because they're well-trained, have sufficient resources, and are placed where they can best use their God-given gifts.
- Parents are informed about what their children are learning and how they can lead faith development and growth at home.
- Communication among volunteers, church staff, and parents is regular, timely, and effective.
- Volunteers connect with parents in a variety of ways (during drop-off and pickup, through take-home materials, by sharing words of praise and encouragement).
- Children and their families see familiar faces in classrooms and at events because volunteers serve consistently.
- Appropriate transitions from one age group to another are planned well and executed consistently.
- Detailed policies and procedures address volunteer screening, safety and security, classroom ratios, emergency procedures, appropriate touch, medical concerns, and cleanliness. A children's ministry director ensures that all staff and volunteers follow these policies and procedures faithfully.
- Learning areas are clean and inviting.

CHAPTER 5

A LEGACY OF FAITH

*T*he purpose and heart of children's ministry is to tell future generations about Jesus. He works through you and blesses you to be a blessing to young people. "But I have only an hour or so with these kids each week," you might be thinking. "How can I make an impact in so little time?"

The final verse of the Bible's shortest book contains five important answers to that question. Third John 1:14 reveals surprisingly simple ways you can share with children the most valuable gift possible: a lasting legacy of faith in Jesus.

"I hope to **see** you soon, and we will **talk face to face**. **Peace** to you. The **friends** here send their greetings. Greet the friends there **by name**" (3 John 1:14).

1. **"See"**—As a volunteer, be the person kids look forward to seeing regularly. Be consistent and reliable, develop appropriate friendships with children, and let them know you're happy to see them. It makes a big difference when kids know you'll be at church waiting for them to arrive and will greet them with a smile.

2. **"Talk face to face"**—Smile, look children in the eyes, and get on their level as you converse with them.

> Always remember that you model Jesus to kids!

29

That might mean sitting on the floor or kneeling for a bit, but it makes communication easier and shows that you care. Kids long for someone at church to really know them and to tell them they're valuable, accepted, and loved. Take time to acknowledge children individually. Don't look past them, and make sure your face doesn't convey impatience, frustration, or disapproval. Always remember that you model Jesus to kids!

3. **"Peace"**—Make your church and children's ministry a refuge. This world can be scary for children, with uncertainty, illness, divorce, financial strain, and violence. Create an environment where kids and parents feel calm and secure. Use security procedures and have a zero-tolerance policy for bullying (yes, that can happen at church).

4. **"Friends"**—Children, especially older ones or those who are visiting your church, return to classes and programs not because of cool videos, crazy skits, fun games, or even your awesome talks. They come back because they have friends there, including you. Videos, skits, and games certainly play a role, but they're simply tools for kids to build relationships with Jesus and with one another. Be intentional about helping children form connections with their peers and teachers.

5. **"By name"**—Every time you meet, address every child by name. (Use name tags!) Be intentional about it so you don't miss anyone; this lets kids know they're each valued as an individual. It's also a game-changer for kids when they hear their name called out in prayer, so regularly pray for each child by name. Take prayer requests from kids, pray together for those requests, and keep track of God's answers.

SECTION 2

THE "WHO" OF CHILDREN'S MINISTRY

CHAPTER 6

A WINNING
CHILDREN'S MINISTRY TEAM

Children's ministry is always a team effort, and people with a wide variety of God-given gifts are needed to keep a program running. The typical program includes people who are willing to provide oversight, handle publicity and communications, plan and teach lessons, greet kids and parents, maintain registration and records, sing, play, drive for field trips, hold babies—and much more! Identifying your talents and strengths helps you find the areas where you can make the biggest contribution and reap the biggest reward.

> Each role is
> equally important

As Paul describes in 1 Corinthians 12, all Christians are part of one body called the church, and each member is equally important. The same holds true for all the positions involved with children's ministry. Each role is equally important, and different people are sure to get excited about different roles. That also adds interest and excitement to volunteering in children's ministry. You have opportunities to work alongside people—both new and familiar to you—who have an assortment of spiritual gifts. Your ministry teammates need you, and you need them. Overseeing it all is the God who distributes those gifts in the first place: "... in everyone it is the same God at work" (1 Corinthians 12:6).

Here's a brief overview of some main roles in children's ministry. For more detailed job descriptions, see chapter 12.

Director

With any church program, someone needs to be in charge. In children's ministry, the director mainly serves in a supervisory role and often spends little or no time in classrooms. Although directors must understand children well and have a passion for reaching them, they spend most of their time organizing, recruiting, training, and appreciating the other team members.

At some churches, the children's ministry director is a paid staff member (either full- or part-time); at others, the director is a volunteer. No matter a church's size, much behind-the-scenes work is necessary to orchestrate an effective program. People who fill director positions tend to prefer administration and organization. They enjoy setting goals and recruiting other teammates who are excited about reaching those goals together.

Teachers

In a children's ministry, teachers do much more than just show up on Sunday mornings. They set the tone for the entire classroom and determine how every session "flows." Teachers commit to preparing and leading each lesson, tailoring it to fit the students in a particular class. Age-level tips provided by the curriculum or director can offer insight into how the children in your care will generally act and think. Of course, over time you'll also want to get to know each child and family on a more personal level.

Anyone filling a teacher role should be comfortable interacting with children and conversing with them at age-appropriate levels. Teachers enjoy helping kids grasp new concepts and ideas, and they're eager to pray with and for them. Teachers are willing to spend time preparing for meaningful, memorable lessons and enjoy seeing children grow in their faith.

Teachers should value their church's basic faith principles. If you've attended for a while, you'll already have a pretty solid grasp of those core beliefs. It's also important to know the ministry's policies and procedures, which may vary according to the ages you teach. As the classroom leader, you need to know emergency plans, bathroom procedures, and other safety and security details. Key topics will be covered in training, orientation, and usually a reference manual too.

Assistant Teachers

These people like to help. Their key roles are making sure all children stay involved with activities and helping in class however necessary.

Assistant teachers read through each lesson beforehand in order to understand the plan and anticipate how they can provide the most aid. They take care of a variety of details, assisting the teacher so class runs smoothly. Examples include setting out craft supplies, debriefing the lesson with a small group of children, helping during games, serving snacks, cleaning up, dealing with any behavioral issues, getting to know parents, and so on. Assistant teachers should be familiar with safety and security procedures so they can help with bathroom visits, emergencies, and fire drills.

Administrative Support

Many people can fill vital behind-the-scenes roles. Positions include helping with registration, overseeing check-in and checkout, taking roll, building sets, handling communications and publicity, updating websites, and more. People gifted in hospitality, creativity, organization, finances, technology, and marketing all are key to a well-run children's ministry.

A reliable, smooth check-in and checkout process, for example, keeps children safe and offers parents peace of mind. These volunteers should be friendly, welcoming, and meticulous at recordkeeping. If the check-in system is electronic, some computer knowledge is helpful.

Someone can take attendance and later walk around to take a headcount, making sure everyone is accounted for. This same person (or another security volunteer) can greet people in the hallways and confirm that they belong there.

Regular communication with parents is vital. If you're a writer, you can volunteer to draft and send weekly emails and monthly newsletters to keep families informed about what's happening in the children's ministry and church. Designers can create publicity pieces to promote fall kickoff festivities, special activities, and important ministry days and events (rally day, Christmas program rehearsals, Easter egg hunts, promotion Sunday, and so on).

If you're a marketer, you can work with the children's ministry director and staff to brainstorm ways to reach the community. Fliers, posters, and door hangers are simple, useful tools for informing and inviting neighbors.

People with organizational skills can keep track of schedules and what's needed in terms of assistance and supplies. Others can organize classrooms and supply areas, restocking supplies as necessary.

If hospitality and cooking are your gifts, you might plan a thank-you event for volunteers once or twice a year. If you enjoy correspondence, your personal touch will be appreciated for sending birthday cards and "We miss you!" notes.

CHAPTER 1

BABIES AND TODDLERS

*M*inistry volunteers who work with very young children have the privilege of igniting the learning process while introducing kids to Jesus. By understanding how God naturally wires babies and toddlers, you gain important perspective plus the skills to foster growth, trust, and confidence in this stage.

> Everyone who provides care for babies is instrumental in giving them a first impression of their heavenly Father.

During the first year of life, infants' inability to take care of themselves produces tension. Babies rely solely on other people, so relationships and experiences shape the way they see the world. There's a direct link between how caregivers respond to a baby's needs and how that child learns to trust others—including God. Everyone who provides care for babies is instrumental in giving them a first impression of their heavenly Father.

Relationships teach babies whether the world is a safe, secure place. When parents and caregivers (including children's ministry volunteers) consistently meet a baby's physical needs, strong attachments form. And as a result of those bonds, young children learn about love and trust.

This chapter offers insights into the characteristics of very young children, as well as how you can effectively minister to them. Because the "babies and toddlers" stage covers a lot of territory, both physically and mentally, let's explore those two categories separately.

Characteristics of Babies

On the surface, the needs of infants appear simple: They sleep a lot, and when they're awake they need to be fed and changed. While babies are being babies, however, so much is going on behind the scenes. At birth, a baby's brain is about one-quarter the size of an adult brain. Amazingly, it doubles in size during the first year of life. By age 3, about 80 percent of the basic brain architecture is wired; by age 5, the brain is almost fully grown.

Newborns have all the brain cells (neurons) they'll have for the rest of their life, but these cells are useless unless they connect with one another and create pathways. Babies spend the next few years making connections and forming pathways as a result of learning. Childhood interactions and relationships, as well as positive and negative experiences, all shape brain development. Everything a baby hears, sees, touches, smells, and tastes stimulates connections that become foundations for future physical, emotional, intellectual, and spiritual development. All these are linked and interdependent, influencing one another.

During this initial stage of life, it's up to the adults who care for babies—and then toddlers—to leverage the unique potential that a growing brain presents. Family members and other caregivers all contribute a strong base for a child's future growth.

Because babies are born with a social drive, human contact is essential for building trust. Infants quickly learn to associate familiar sights, sounds, smells, and touch with security. Volunteer as consistently as possible so little ones in the church nursery feel safe and loved through familiarity. Avoid loud noises and quick movements, wear soft clothing, and maintain a cheerful attitude.

With each passing day, an infant's muscles strengthen and the nervous system matures, allowing babies to gain control over their bodies. New skills abound in the first year of life: lifting the head and chest, reaching for objects, rolling over, crawling, standing unsupported, and eventually walking. Each new physical milestone sets the stage for the next, sparking intellectual, emotional, and spiritual developments.

Babies' vision isn't yet 20/20, and their world is two-dimensional. They see objects best when they're about a foot away. Help sharpen their vision by letting them stare at your face and at objects with high contrast.

During the first year, language outpaces almost all other areas of development. Infants are born with the unique ability to absorb and distinguish speech sounds rapidly in their first few months. Babies long to hear familiar voices and learn to trust them. When you're in the nursery, talk to them often so your voice becomes a recognizable source of comfort and trust.

Structure helps babies thrive and feel secure. Although routines may be tough to implement in the nursery initially, over time they help little ones feel safe and help you minister most effectively—and when babies' brains are most receptive. A solid nursery routine includes songs, stories, and prayers, plus structured and unstructured play times. When routines are interrupted, babies may act up.

At six months, memory begins to develop. Babies can remember how important their primary caregivers are to them and feel anxious when those people they rely on are out of sight. We give babies a glimpse of God's love by respecting their need to feel safe rather than forcing them to just "get over" their anxiety.

Babies store both positive and negative memories, recalling them based on brain connections made by using their five senses. Allowing babies to cry repeatedly for long periods of time can cause them to associate negative feelings with a certain room or caregivers. That, in turn, increases fear produced by separation anxiety. Every nursery should have a policy about this; for example, paging parents after about five minutes of inconsolable crying.

Security objects such as blankets and soft toys are often part of a growing baby's support system. These "loveys" comfort babies when they're frightened, help them sleep when they're tired, provide reassurance when they're separated from caregivers, and help them feel at home when they're in a strange place. In short, security objects help babies make the emotional transition from dependence to independence.

When babies drop toys, scream, or act in other undesirable ways, they're not necessarily being defiant. They're merely conducting "experiments" that stimulate various brain circuits. You can learn to take cues from these actions to provide an environment that lights up those circuits yet minimizes your frustrations. Use the power of a hug, gentle touch, or calm voice to guide babies. Look into their eyes while talking to them, and always use positive words.

> Every baby is "fearfully and wonderfully made" (Psalm 139:14), so each one has unique needs.

Every baby is "fearfully and wonderfully made" (Psalm 139:14), so each one has unique needs. Observe and cater to their preferences. Pray for discernment and ask God to multiply your influence while babies are in your care.

Teaching Tips

Make the most of one-to-one moments with each baby in your care. Slow down, make eye contact, and interact using facial expressions as well as your voice. Babies are sponges and experience the world through their senses. Help them see, hear, smell, feel, and taste the goodness of our God—and of everything he has made.

Repetition helps strengthen brain circuits, so repeat simple phrases and baby's name often. For example, say "God made (baby's name)," "God loves (baby's name)," "God knows (baby's name) from the top of her head to the bottom of her toes." Babies will learn these powerful truths and associate them with you and the church.

Babies perfect skills by imitating people. Structure Bible songs and activities to include clapping, crawling, reaching, grasping, and pointing—and let little ones copy you. Sing songs about God's love and care. Personalize lyrics by inserting baby's name. Throughout the room, post Bible verses that you can read aloud to babies as you walk around with them. Read simple and colorful Bible storybooks. Personalize the story by inserting each baby's name, when possible.

To pray with babies, hold them tenderly, use their names, and pray over them both aloud and silently. Pray for their faith, their family and caretakers, the ability to trust, safety, purity, future, character, and friendships.

Keep lessons simple and tactile. For example, when teaching on the topic of Creation, you can collect 10 small, creation-related objects and place each in a separate box or bag (one per baby). To reduce distractions, bring out one box at a time, keeping the others out of sight. Do the following simple activities back to back without pausing, spending two or three minutes with each object. End every activity by asking babies to put items back in the box.

- **Children's Bibles or Bible storybooks**—Give each baby a small Bible to hold. Together, sing "The B-I-B-L-E." Then take turns sharing this truth with every child: "The Bible says God created everything, including (child's name)."
- **Small toy birds**—Give each baby a bird and say, "God made birds." Show babies how to fly birds in the air while making bird sound effects. Say, "God made birds to fly in the sky."
- **Small baby dolls**—As you hand each baby a doll, say, "God made babies. God made (baby's name)." Point to various parts of the doll and say, "God

made your eyes, ears, mouth...." When it's time to put away the dolls, collect them from babies one at a time and say, "God loves (baby's name)." For this activity, you can use baby-safe, handheld mirrors instead of dolls.

- **Fresh flowers**—Hand each baby a flower (or petal) and say, "God made flowers. They are soft and pretty. They smell sweet." Demonstrate how babies can gently feel and smell the flowers.

Other objects that work well for this type of interactive learning include globe balls, toy animals and fish, toy food, and small plastic bottles filled with dirt or water. The list is endless! Websites such as Oriental Trading offer a variety of inexpensive items. Repeat these activities every week. You might get bored, but babies thrive on repetition and routine.

Classroom Space

Babies need room to explore in a safe, controlled environment. Designate plenty of space for crawlers and new walkers. Create areas with bright colors, comfortable furniture, and stimulating objects. Keep the area smelling fresh, and play soft music with Bible lyrics.

Stock the nursery with toys that spur brain connections and create opportunities for trial-and-error learning. Stuffed animals, big soft blocks, objects with mirrors, stacking rings, shape sorters, and push toys are great ways to stimulate learning and development. You can include various toys in your Bible activities and stories.

Other must-have items for a nursery include a secured and safe changing table, diaper receptacle, rocking chair, walker, swing, and evacuation crib. If possible, invest in a table with bucket seats. It frees up volunteers to engage babies in structured activities.

Characteristics of Toddlers

During the second year of life, a child's growing need for autonomy causes tension. As toddlers develop physical, mental, and emotional skills, they discover they have a personality, complete with their own desires and abilities. Adults, meanwhile, try to cope with this emerging individuality and independence. By actively nurturing toddlers' need for autonomy, we help them gain confidence, which leads to a positive self-image. On the other hand, dampening their efforts can contribute to feelings of shame. So it's important to help toddlers feel encouraged and hopeful.

Accept the fact that this is the "me do it!" stage. Most toddlers are determined to complete tasks, such as feeding and dressing themselves, without assistance. Expect messes and spills. Praise toddlers for their smallest efforts, and show them acceptable ways to express frustration.

Expect toddlers to be active! As they climb, jump, hop, skip, touch, manipulate objects, and explore the world using all five senses, children discover their abilities as well as the relationship between actions and consequences.

> Imagination is a powerful tool to introduce toddlers to God.

Most toddlers are wired with a vivid imagination, which boosts self-esteem and helps them experiment with their own thoughts, feelings, and ideas. If harnessed, imagination is a powerful tool to introduce toddlers to God.

Toddlers also need the freedom to safely make choices without constant correction. Provide opportunities for children to observe, sort, solve problems, and learn from their mistakes. Refrain from harsh criticism and unrealistic expectations, which negatively impact self-esteem in the long run. Instead, offer affirmations such as "You did it!" "You're okay," "You're a good listener," and "Thanks for being a helper!"

Teaching Tips

Create a schedule that satisfies toddlers' natural inquisitiveness. Include times for talking, reading, singing, playing, and eating snacks. Brain development is "activity-dependent," meaning toddlers are designed to do things that trigger and satisfy sensory, motor, emotional, and intellectual curiosities.

Toddlers listen to your words closely, so use simple language and a soft tone. Share personalized biblical truths; for example, "God made (toddler's name)," "God loves (toddler's name)," and "Jesus wants to be (toddler's name) best friend forever."

Read aloud Bible storybooks that have colorful illustrations. After sharing a simple Bible story, encourage toddlers to review it by acting it out. Imaginative role-play allows children to become part of God's unfolding story with a sense of innocence that adults lose. Avoid structure and correction. It's okay if multiple kids want to play the same character or if they embellish the story.

Sing short, repetitive songs such as "Jesus Loves Me," and play kid-friendly worship music during crafts and playtime. Also provide space for toddlers to dance, without insisting that movements be done in a certain way.

Pray with toddlers by saying, "God, please help us know your Son, Jesus," "God, thank you for (point to items or pictures) ...," "God, please help me ..."

To promote learning and avoid boredom, frustration, and behavioral issues, use a milestone chart to select age-appropriate activities. To avoid distractions, stick to one activity at a time. Toddlers need to engage all their senses to focus and maximize learning from each activity. Removing all background busyness during structured times helps reduce overstimulation, irritability, and distractions. This might mean turning off a video or music and asking all volunteers to engage in the activity.

Because toddlers can act up when moving to a new activity, signal transitions ahead of time. By announcing, "I'm putting away this storybook" before actually doing it, you prepare children and also teach them cause and effect.

If the classroom becomes chaotic, find nurturing ways to regain control. Don't underestimate the power of a hug, gentle touch, or calm voice. Look into children's eyes while talking to them, and always use positive words. Avoid phrases such as "you didn't" and "you shouldn't."

Here are some examples of how you can teach toddlers about Creation (building off the ideas from earlier in this chapter):

- Create a landscape in a long rectangular tub or box. Seat toddlers around it, and let them dig in the dirt, plant a seed, pick up small rocks, smell a flower, and touch a plant. Play nature sounds in the background. Talk about how God made all things, including each of us.

- Fill a water table or tub with water. Let toddlers dig for shells, play with boats, and handle objects that float or sink. Give them a few cups to fill with water and empty. Play water sounds in the background. Discuss how God created water and how water is used (to drink, to bathe, to swim and splash, for water creatures to live in).

- Make reusable sensory bags. Fill a large zippered baggie with kid-safe colored hair gel and add soft, colorful items related to the Creation account (squishy frogs or fish, plastic flowers or leaves, wiggle eyes). Remove extra air, seal the baggie, and reinforce all the sides with colored duct tape. As you share the Creation story, let children see, feel, and squeeze objects in the baggie.

Classroom Space and Management

Fill your meeting area with engaging, developmentally appropriate toys. These include peg puzzles, shape sorters, jumbo crayons, stacking toys, trucks, dolls, trains, pretend food, soft balls, soft blocks, and dress-up clothes.

Provide art supplies so toddlers can express themselves in a variety of ways. Set out modeling clay or crayons, and then listen as children talk about what they're making. Rejoice and celebrate their creativity, and find opportunities to link their abstract masterpieces to the day's lesson.

Provide spaces and latitude for toddlers to repeatedly fail safely. When they fall or struggle, use encouraging words and hugs. To minimize constant correction that leads to shame and self-doubt, child-proof the area by adding safety latches, covering outlets, and removing unsafe furniture that's tempting to climb.

Partnering with Parents of Babies and Toddlers

No one has a greater influence on babies and toddlers than their parents. By partnering with moms and dads and keeping them well-informed, children's ministry staff and volunteers strengthen the foundation of homes and bless the church.

Help parents discern what's critical for spiritual formation. Parents are bombarded with a wide array of parenting advice via magazines, television, social media, friends, and family. Plus, they're often dealing with sleeplessness and jam-packed schedules, so the idea of adding one more responsibility can be discouraging and stressful. That's why Deuteronomy 6:4-9 exhorts parents to model their love for God during daily routines, which becomes a catalyst in building faith at home. Provide simple resources that equip parents to create teachable moments during meals, playtime, and travel time. Emphasize the necessity of repeating activities frequently to create stronger brain connections.

Celebrate spiritual milestones. Help parents anticipate, prepare for, and mark the next stage of their child's faith life. Depending on the traditions your church observes, milestones may include infant dedication or baptism, a child's first Bible, and eventually a public profession of faith or confirmation and first communion. Educate parents about the concepts of each mile marker, and offer practical tools for actively nurturing faith during each stage.

> Help parents anticipate, prepare for, and mark the next stage of their child's faith life.

Offer "felt-need" classes. Every developmental stage brings new skills to learn—for children as well as parents. Ask an expert from your church or community to offer some workshops on baby's first year, nutrition, toilet training, discipline, and other topics. Include a biblical component, such as devotion time and prayer, plus social time for parents to interact.

Create a support network. Provide parents with godly mentors, such as older couples or grandparents, who can share wisdom and offer encouragement. A faith-based support system will remind parents to follow the instructions in God's Word, not the whims of secular culture. Host events such as picnics, playdates, and Parents Day Out so moms and dads can connect with one another, enjoy some down time, and meet their children's friends from church and Sunday school.

Request inside information. In addition to registration forms and emergency contact cards, have parents complete a questionnaire about how their babies prefer to be held, soothed, fed, rocked, and laid down in a crib when sleepy. At pickup, build trust by providing feedback about a baby's time in the nursery. And when it's time to transition to the toddler room, involve parents to gain understanding—and to prepare volunteers—about how their baby might react.

CHAPTER 8

PRESCHOOLERS
AND KINDERGARTNERS

*T*eaching God's Word to young children is both a privilege and a responsibility. As a representative of Jesus and a spiritual role model, you provide an important first impression of what God's people are like. Be prayerful as you plan, teach, and interact with every child and parent. Make every effort to reflect the character of Christ and the fruit of the Spirit (see Galatians 5:22-23).

As a volunteer, you can take some simple steps to be a good church friend and leader to preschoolers and kindergartners. Create an atmosphere where learning and interaction are relational. Get to know kids collectively and also as unique individuals. Call them by name. Listen to them and learn what's important to each of them. Get down on the children's level and maintain eye contact. Don't be afraid to play with the children and be silly. Choose words and actions that show them they're safe, loved, and accepted at church. Be patient, warm, friendly, and offer physical touch in appropriate ways (high five, pat on the back, side hug). Let kids lead in this area, never forcing a child to give or return affection.

No matter your role as a volunteer, make prayer a cornerstone of your ministry. Pray for children by name, before teaching and throughout the week. Find a system that works for you, such as keeping a class roll in your Bible, using a monthly prayer guide, adding children's names to Bible verses as prayers, and so on. Occasionally send a postcard or message to families, letting them know you've been praying for them, especially if they've shared specific requests.

Also remember to pray for your ministry and yourself. Make prayer an important part of your weekly preparation. Thank God for entrusting you with such an important and rewarding role. Seek God's will as you plan, trusting him to give you discernment, creativity, confidence, flexibility, and a positive attitude. Ask Jesus to help you reflect his love to the children by extending patience, grace, and attention. Commit your plans to the Lord (see Proverbs 16:3), and ask him to help you love and serve each child as he does.

Characteristics of Preschoolers and Kindergartners

Between the ages of 3 and 6, children undergo many changes. They experience rapid physical growth, learn vast amounts of knowledge, and quickly acquire new skills. Preschoolers and kindergartners primarily learn through play, often by imitating the significant adults in their lives. Amid all this activity, children become more and more independent. Let's take a closer look at the characteristics of preschoolers and kindergartners.

During this stage, children gain confidence through increasingly complex movements (hopping, skipping, balancing on one foot, and walking backward). Although kids still require significant physical activity, they're also developing fine motor skills such as drawing, working puzzles, cutting with scissors, building with smaller blocks, and even printing words. Older preschoolers and kindergartners start to display right-handedness or left-handedness, show hand-eye coordination, and lose their baby teeth.

Mentally, preschoolers and kindergartners are curious and imaginative. They're proud of their age, size, and abilities, and they're eager to share their knowledge and display their skills. These children ask many "how?" and "why?" questions. Because they're still concrete thinkers, they can't separate fantasy from reality or reason logically, and they don't fully comprehend the concept of time.

In general, preschoolers and kindergartners have an attention span of one minute per year of life, meaning a 5-year-old has a five-minute attention span. These children enjoy role-play, have a growing vocabulary, can sort and match items, recognize words, and some are even beginning to read.

Emotionally and socially, 3- to 6-year-olds have a growing sense of independence and confidence in their abilities, yet the adults in their lives still have great influence. Young children are eager to please and generally believe what they're told. During this stage, kids move from parallel play (playing alongside each other) to cooperative play (learning to share and take turns, work with others, and follow simple game rules).

Children also are developing morally. They tend to be motivated by rules and often rely on external clues to determine if something is right or wrong. They're discovering that consequences have actions, yet they still have a tough time seeing things from someone else's perspective. Self-control remains a challenge. A preschooler will experience shame and guilt, but the conscience is just beginning to develop.

Spiritually, preschoolers know the Bible is a special book and enjoy hearing stories from it. They're capable of identifying some Bible characters, retelling some Bible stories, memorizing simple verses, and singing songs about God. They often imitate the religious actions of their parents and teachers; for example, they may pray using the same words and postures they see modeled and want to bring their own Bible to church. These are critical years for instilling God's Word in young minds and hearts.

Teaching Tips

Teaching God's Word to preschoolers and kindergartners—while helping them develop trust in church leaders—is an exciting and rewarding responsibility. The most important part of your time with children is sharing a Bible story and verse, discussing life applications, and praying together.

For each lesson, choose a simple, age-appropriate Bible truth. Here are some examples:

- God made the world and everything in it, including people.
- God is good and loves all people.
- The Bible is God's Word to us, and everything it says is true.
- Jesus is God's Son.
- Jesus always obeyed God.
- Jesus loves me.
- God is with me and helps me.
- At church, we worship God by singing, listening to Bible stories, and talking to God.
- God wants family members to love and help one another.

Children can verbalize these truths before they really understand them. At this age, kids typically don't yet think abstractly, so it can be difficult for them to grasp more symbolic aspects of faith. Because preschoolers learn through play, select a variety of activities, games, crafts, and songs to reinforce each week's message.

> Identify the main point and repeat it often.

Use a "less is more" approach, keeping lessons simple. Identify the main point and repeat it often. It's better for children to truly comprehend and apply one key point than to hear vast amounts of Scripture they won't remember. Repetition is a wonderful technique, because it allows young children to practice new skills and predict what will happen next. Hearing or doing the same thing over and over may seem boring to adults, but it's exciting for 3- to 6-year-olds and builds their self-confidence.

Children retain knowledge better when they make discoveries, so select learning-center activities and games that provide opportunities for movement and experiences. Learning about Jesus becomes fun for young children when leaders encourage wonder and accommodate their need to move and wiggle. Choose tasks that are simple enough for kids to be successful, engage as many senses as possible, and use gross motor skills (bigger movements) as well as fine motor skills. Make play meaningful by connecting each engaging activity with God's Word. As children work and play, repeat the lesson's Bible truth and relate it—and their actions—to their daily lives.

During group time, include as much variety as possible. Because preschoolers and kindergartners have such a brief attention span, you'll probably need to recapture their

> Include as much variety as possible.

interest every few minutes by changing activities or presentation techniques. Keep lessons as interactive as possible, remembering to use simple vocabulary. Add variety with these techniques:

- **Storytelling**—Children love a great storyteller! Be familiar enough with the Bible lesson that you can tell it, not read it. Even better, use different voices for each character. Create interest by changing your pitch and volume. Throughout the story, repeat a word or phrase multiple times that children can say along with you. If numbers are part of the lesson or can be worked into it, invite kids to join you in counting.

- **Visual aids**—Give children something to focus on as you teach. Show a poster of the Bible story, use a flannel board with Bible-character cutouts, interact with a puppet, or bring props to accompany the lesson. To help children separate fact from fiction, always hold an open Bible in your lap as you discuss lessons from God's Word.

- **Mystery**—Tell children you have a surprise for them at the end of the story. Show them a bag with a mystery item inside, hold something behind your back, or tell them something is hidden in the room. Make sure the mystery relates to the daily Bible truth. The suspense maintains children's interest.

- **Participation**—Keep children engaged and their hands busy. Have them make sounds, hand motions, or facial expressions. Guide them to act out the story as you tell it—or to act like animals mentioned. They can "hee-haw" every time you say "donkey," make a fish face when you say "fish," pat their legs when a character walks down the road, and so on. Adding hand motions to Bible verses and songs makes memorization easier.

- **Music**—When you incorporate music and sounds, children hear the Bible lesson in a new way. Use sound effects as you tell the story, or sing the Bible verse to a familiar tune. Throughout your teaching, intersperse simple worship songs.

- **Games**—Play games that help children recall what they've learned. Give clues and let them guess which animal you're describing. Pass a ball around the circle as music plays. Stop the music and ask the child who's holding the ball to name one thing Jesus does. For a lesson about David caring for sheep, hide cotton balls around the room for kids to find and gather.

As you try various techniques, gauge children's interest and then repeat, shift gears, or wrap up as needed. Keep in mind that children learn in many different ways, so try to accommodate all learning styles: visual, auditory, reading/writing, and kinesthetic. Almost all preschoolers and kindergartners are kinesthetic (or tactile) learners, meaning they learn best by moving and doing. For information about even more "intelligences," see chapter 14.

During lessons, pray with children often. Teach them that prayer is simply talking to God, and they can do it anytime and anywhere. Remind kids the Bible tells us God listens when we pray. Model prayer, showing that we close our eyes and bow our heads to show respect for God. Because children learn by doing, invite them to pray with you and on their own. Make a simple prayer song part of your snack time routine. During life-application time, say a prayer one phrase at a time, allowing the group to repeat each phrase. Pray about what's important to children. Provide opportunities for kids to pray aloud, but never force someone to do so.

Classroom Space and Management

A clean, safe environment is essential for learning, but it's just the start. When setting up your classroom, also consider purpose and functionality. Begin by identifying a spot for group time. This is where children gather for a Bible story, songs, and group games. The space should be large enough for kids to sit in a circle with you, possibly on a rug or on individual carpet squares. It's also helpful to have a focal wall, white board, or bulletin board for visual aids.

The next priority is creating spaces for learning centers. Children can rotate through interactive stations, experiencing a hands-on activity at each one. Common learning centers for preschoolers and kindergartners include home living, dramatic play, books and quiet space, blocks and construction, art, manipulatives and puzzles, and nature and science. Four learning centers per session is sufficient, and it's best to have no more than four or five children at each station at once. Rather than including the "books and quiet space" center as a planned rotation, you can reserve that area for one or two children at a time who may need a break from noise, activity, or their own emotions. Think carefully about which centers you position near one another or by doors and certain furniture. Also be considerate of other leaders and ministries who may use the room throughout the week. At learning centers, it's helpful to limit toy choices. Too many can be overwhelming for young children and time-consuming to clean up.

Carefully determine a general schedule and follow it consistently. Preschoolers and kindergartners appreciate routine and predictability, so knowing what to expect feels reassuring to them. Plan to spend the majority of classroom time in learning centers. Also include time for arrival and opening activities, group time, crafts, games, cleanup, and any other components deemed necessary.

> Encourage children's sense of wonder and their desire to explore and create.

Despite the importance of routine, it's also important to stay flexible and celebrate childhood. Don't become so attached to a set schedule that you rush kids who are enjoying an activity or miss an opportunity for relationship-building moments. Encourage children's sense of wonder and their desire to explore and create. Today's kids are pushed to grow up quickly. Allow church—and, specifically, your classroom—to be a place where they're heard and not rushed.

Set up young children for success by planning activities they can complete with minimal or no assistance. Give simple directions and repeat them as needed. Offer kids a sense of purpose by asking them to help with classroom jobs. They can hold the Bible story picture during group time, bring crayons to the craft tables, hand out napkins for snack, and so on.

Make the most of every moment spent with children and families at the classroom door. If possible, provide consistency by having the same person greet families every week. Children and parents will look forward to seeing a familiar face. As kids arrive, position yourself to be on their level and welcome them by name. This initial encounter sets the tone for your time together, so be positive with your words, expressions, and attitude. Warmly greet parents too, but focus on the child transitioning into the room smoothly. If the child has food or a personal toy, try to leave it with parents or put it away until departure time. Ask parents to label children's belongings and keep them together in bags or cubbies. Help parents understand it's best to say a quick goodbye in the hallway rather than entering the classroom with their child.

When the session is wrapping up, encourage children to continue activities so they're not watching the door and anxiously waiting for parents. When a child is picked up, briefly share with parents a positive word about something their child did or learned. If a behavioral issue or other concern needs to be discussed, it's best to talk with a parent later, when the child and other families aren't present. Keep your time at the door light and affirming.

Behavioral Issues

Because preschoolers and kindergartners are still developing self-control, they may not always act angelic during Sunday school! But your focus should be on lovingly guiding children's actions, not on punishing them. Young children are in the process of learning to honor and obey God, parents, and teachers.

It's important to maintain realistic expectations and to communicate those expectations clearly. Each child is different and develops at a unique pace physically, mentally, and spiritually, so don't make comparisons. Young children often become frustrated with difficult tasks or overwhelmed by their emotions. Extend patience, grace, and love as you guide them.

- Use these tips to address behavioral issues:
- Be proactive and try to avoid problems *before* they arise. Be prepared, arrive early, and begin activities right away to avoid idleness, which often leads to unwanted behavior.
- Eliminate distractions. Avoid activities that overstimulate children and toys that are particularly difficult to share.
- Create a few classroom rules that are easy for children to understand and obey; for example, be kind, use inside voices, and listen to others. Refer to these rules often in a cheerful voice. Set an example with your own tone and behavior, using good manners and following the rules.
- Use positive reinforcement by praising children for obedience and good choices. Preschoolers and kindergartners hear "don't" and "no" often, so use positive instructions as much as possible; for example, say, "Please walk" instead of "Don't run."
- To hold children's attention and keep them on task, use attention-getters; for example, clap your hands, sing a song, or repeat a happy phrase. Young children are most likely to lose control during transition times.
- Separate children who are likely to misbehave when together, and position leaders near kids who struggle with self-control.
- When choosing words and consequences, prioritize safety and relationship with the child. Most

discipline issues can be dealt with calmly within the classroom. Overlook small infractions that aren't disrespectful or harmful. However, if actions put the child or others in immediate danger (hitting, kicking, throwing, biting, etc.), quickly remove the child from the room and contact parents for pickup.

- In cases of disrespect or disobedience, first try to alter the child's actions through distraction and gentle reminders of expected behavior. If the issue continues, use a timeout (one minute per each year of the child's age). If you feel yourself becoming angry or frustrated, ask an assistant to help.

- Never scold or shame a child, and don't draw undue attention to someone. During group time, it's best for an assistant—or a teacher who isn't leading at the moment—to address behavioral issues.

- Intentionally express God's love and refer to God's Word. Behavioral issues often lead to one-on-one conversations with children, creating special opportunities to connect with them. Move with the child to a quiet area of the room. Use a soft, calm voice to remind the child of your love—and God's. Briefly discuss what actions weren't acceptable, offering a related Bible truth as encouragement. Pray with the child, asking God for help to make good choices.

Partnering with Parents

When the church works with families for children's well-being, everyone benefits. You can do that by extending an attitude of grace, praying for parents regularly, providing Bible-based parenting resources, and supporting them as they invest in their children's spiritual development. Each week, provide a copy of the Bible lesson, along with conversation starters so families can keep talking at home. Some parents may feel uncertain about their ability to be spiritual leaders. Make it clear that your purpose isn't to replace or belittle parents but to encourage and equip them. Parents and other family members need help and support, not judgment!

One of the most humbling and special aspects of working with preschoolers and kindergartners is being welcomed into their family's lives. Trust is built through connections, and you'll quickly earn the privilege of celebrating and mourning with them, hearing their needs and struggles, and being asked for prayer and advice. During all that, you can point families to Jesus.

As you're able, minister to families during special occasions or struggles. Ideas include delivering a gift or meal when a baby is born or adopted, sending a note or offering to babysit when a loved one dies, and making a bag of activities for the hospital when a child has a medical procedure or overnight stay. Ask parents who've experienced a miscarriage, a special-needs diagnosis, or an extended NICU stay if you can connect them with a pastor or with others walking a similar path.

Christian community is a gift to families, so encourage relationships and foster friendships. Plan family events, introduce families with common needs or interests, and suggest simple service opportunities. Plan a playdate at a local park for fun and fellowship. When a new family visits the church, introduce them to others in the congregation—especially those with children of similar ages.

As you connect with parents, remember to include *all* families, regardless of race, socio-economic level, marital status, special needs, etc. Recognize that some children are being raised by grandparents or other family members and some are in foster care.

Create personal boundaries for yourself and respect the boundaries of others. Also check your motives to ensure you're working to point people to Jesus, not to build a fan base for yourself.

Connecting with parents is a fantastic way to champion families, point them to Jesus, and ultimately grow God's kingdom.

CHAPTER 9

LOWER-ELEMENTARY CHILDREN (FIRST- TO THIRD-GRADERS)

*Q*uestions, energy, new discoveries, friendships, and genuine faith—these are just some of the exciting aspects of working with first- through third-graders. In other words, it's never boring!

The transition from kindergarten to elementary school is exciting for children as well as for their families. Kids become more independent and no longer need constant supervision. They also become more curious and adept at back-and-forth conversations.

Although first- through third-graders experience many cognitive and social changes, they still have childlike innocence. As a children's ministry volunteer, you can gradually introduce more complex biblical truths as kids learn to reason, differentiate fact from fantasy, and discover how God's Word applies to them personally. Instead of regurgitating what children have heard before, you can add more depth and help young learners take important new steps in their spiritual walk. First, it's important to understand what makes these kids tick.

Characteristics of Lower-Elementary Children (First- to Third-Graders)

Although children in this age group are still energetic, with each year they develop longer and longer attention spans. Being in a school setting increases their ability to sit in a controlled learning environment. That doesn't mean you need to mimic weekday classrooms, but you'll notice that kids stay a bit more focused during lessons and activities.

Children in lower-elementary grades are learning machines. Compared to kindergartners, they can absorb more details, follow instructions better, and begin working with others. After setting a few guidelines and boundaries, you can give children creative freedom to tackle projects independently. This is exciting because with all their different gifts and learning styles (see chapter 14), they can experience and express faith in more personal ways. Lower-elementary children begin to discover who they are as individuals, and the church is a great place for them to see who God created them to be.

According to psychologist Jean Piaget's theory of cognitive development, children ages 7 to 11 are in the "concrete operational" stage. They begin to demonstrate logical reasoning and can consider other people's perspectives. Because these children are becoming thinkers and reasoners, they're ready to start discussing and grappling with truths they may have already heard countless times. But because they're still concrete thinkers, it's important to build bridges from concepts they already understand to some of the more abstract aspects of faith. That reinforces a strong foundation for future development.

In early elementary school, most children are able to read, though it's important to be mindful of those who struggle with this skill. Reading opens new doors to learning, as kids no longer have to rely on what they hear others read and teach. Being able to explore God's Word themselves adds validity to biblical truths and lets curious kids expand their study on their own.

At this stage, children understand the concept of time and the difference between now and long ago. As a result, the sequence of biblical events and how they relate to one another takes shape. Kids also understand cause and effect, opening a new door to how

Bible stories impact their lives. And they begin to grasp the use of religious rituals and even symbolism.

By elementary school, children recognize right from wrong. During Bible lessons, they can tell who obeys or disobeys God's commands. Although this is great knowledge for behavioral modification, that's not the goal of children's ministry. Teachers present the truth of the Gospel and then allow the Holy Spirit to work in young hearts. God reveals to children that they are sinners who need a Savior. Instead of trying harder, they only need to accept Jesus' free gift of salvation. "But God demonstrates his own love for us in this: While we were still sinners, Christ died for us" (Romans 5:8).

This central concept of Christianity begins to sink in during this stage. Children can learn that Jesus rescues us from sin and death—and lives in our hearts. They also start to see how Jesus' friends and followers (i.e., Christians) respond to his love by trusting him, obeying him, and telling others about him.

It's important to remember that these kids are, in fact, kids. They'll test boundaries, question things they've been told, and sometimes make reactionary decisions. That's why they need loving adults to come alongside them, teaching and modeling the Christian faith.

Teaching Tips

> There's a big difference between knowing biblical truths and embracing them through life application.

Elementary-age children can learn many facts, but there's a big difference between knowing biblical truths and embracing them through life application. In other words, the ability to recite Bible facts—or even Bible verses—isn't the same as having a personal faith.

Present every lesson through a Gospel-centered filter. In children's ministry, effective teaching starts and ends with truths from God's Word. Don't overlook certain truths because you're unsure if children can grasp them or because you're afraid some topics aren't "kid-friendly" enough. The world is full of lies, and Satan doesn't water down his attack on children. So why would we water down scriptural truths for kids?

- Children in lower-elementary grades need to regularly hear the Gospel's life-changing message. They can comprehend truths such as:
- God the Father created us and is in charge of the world.
- All people have sinned, and sin has consequences (Romans 3:23; 6:23).
- Heaven and hell are real places.
- By dying on the cross and rising from the dead, Jesus (God the Son) forgives our sins. Through Jesus' sacrifice for us, we can live with him forever in heaven.
- God the Holy Spirit lives in our hearts to help us follow Jesus and share our faith with other people.

Curriculum lessons may focus on Bible "heroes" such as Moses, Rahab, Esther, David, or Paul, but it's important to emphasize that these real-life people were fallen sinners just like us. Only through God's power did they contribute to his greater plan of redemption. Guard against presenting Bible truths as a bunch of separate, feel-good accounts; instead, connect each one to the best news ever—Jesus' death and resurrection.

Foster good communication and interaction. As part of the larger body of Christ, kids need to deepen their faith while

> As part of the larger body of Christ, kids need to deepen their faith while growing closer to their peers.

growing closer to their peers. Working in groups and making discoveries alongside other kids helps grow faith as well as friendships. Helping kids make connections at church *now* gives them the gift of a faith community for the future, too.

Interactive learning is key because it boosts memory and recall. It's easier to remember something we've experienced than something we've merely heard. Encourage kids to become part of each lesson through discussions, drama, games, crafts, and more. Questions also play a vital role in learning, and lower-elementary children are inquisitive by nature.

Throughout his earthly ministry, Jesus uses questions to teach truths, search hearts, and get to the core of people's beliefs. Children may get used to feeding teachers what they think we want to hear. So, take time to ask what they've learned, what they do and don't understand, and what they believe. Then allow plenty of opportunities—and a safe place—for kids to ask questions. Encourage them to grapple with new or challenging concepts so you can point them to God's Word for answers. After all, it's much better for kids to seek answers inside the church than out in the world.

Admit that you're still growing in your faith, too—and be sure to *keep* growing! Don't feel pressure to always have instant answers to children's questions. If you're stumped, be honest and say so. Explain that you'll look in the Bible or ask a pastor. If an answer isn't found, explain that sometimes here on earth we don't have all the answers, but we can trust God, who does. After all, "faith is confidence in what we hope for and assurance about what we do not see" (Hebrews 11:1).

> If you're stumped, be honest and say so.

Remind kids that you, too, are a sinner who needs Jesus and his forgiveness, grace, and strength. Children need to see their adult leaders reading the Bible, praying, attending corporate worship, giving, serving, and applying God's Word to their lives.

Praying with Children

Hearing children talk to their heavenly Father is an amazing sound. At this stage, kids tend to be honest and open. In your ministry, provide a secure setting to learn to pray--whether it involves praying silently, praying aloud, or wrestling with God in prayer. Just make sure you don't spend more time talking about prayer than actually praying!

With lower-elementary children, these prayer models work well:

- The Lord's Prayer
- ACTS (**A**doration, **C**onfession, **T**hanksgiving, **S**upplication)
- CHAT (**C**heer on God for who he is, **H**umble yourself before God, **A**ppreciate what God has done, and **T**ell God your needs)

With an energetic group, interactive prayer is especially effective. The Bible doesn't say we must pray while sitting perfectly still, with hands folded and head bowed. Think creatively as you help kids practice talking and listening to God. Try prayer stations, different postures, and ideas such as popcorn prayer (with kids shouting out a word or phrase that comes to mind).

Remember to conduct prayer follow-up, too. When children bring requests before God, it's important to reflect on his answers, whether "yes," "no," or "not now." You can keep a class prayer journal to help kids see that God hears and answers our prayers.

Classroom Management

A successful learning environment has predictable routines and clear expectations. At the outset, explain how you expect children to act, participate, and treat others. By first grade, children can be involved in setting classroom rules. Giving kids some age-appropriate ownership helps them understand why things are done a certain way and shows them how to be part of the solution, not part of the problem.

Most first- through third-graders are natural pleasers; they intuitively want to follow the rules and be seen (and praised) as obedient. Although the concept of "law" is a must for classroom management, in a church setting it's also important to demonstrate the Gospel truth of grace. As Romans 3:23 says, we're all sinners; that means children will disobey, no matter how carefully you plan. Always responding with rigid legalism leaves no room for God's mercy, which he offers freely to all who ask. Sometimes it might be fitting to not give children a consequence they deserve, or to let them stay in class even when they act up.

The "three-strikes" rule is a handy method for this age group. The first time a child breaks a classroom rule, the leader gives a warning and some type of behavior correction. After the second offense, the leader takes the child aside to discuss the problem. This is a great time to ask questions, inquiring if the child understands why the behavior isn't in the group's best interest. During this second-strike step, take time to pray with the child. Together, ask Jesus for wisdom to make better choices.

A third infraction presents an opportunity for the leader to address behavior with a child's parent. During a private discussion, reinforce that the child is welcome and important to the class, but seek ways the parent can support your efforts. Ask for ideas that may have worked with the child in another setting, such as weekday school or daycare.

With the three-strikes rule, it's essential that each child begins the new week with a clean slate, no matter what may have happened previously.

While working with younger children, remember the importance of helping them understand how to repent and how to ask for and grant forgiveness. The goal of classroom-management techniques isn't perfect children; after all, that's unattainable. The goal is to shine a spotlight on the Gospel and our need for a Savior. When children engage in behaviors that don't honor God, gently and lovingly pointing them to the cross can have a powerful impact.

Thankfully, it's not up to us and our top-notch programs and lessons to work in children's hearts. Instead, we can rely on the Holy Spirit and yield to *his* powerful, mysterious work on young hearts. Pray that God will help you guard against any conscious or subconscious manipulation in children's spiritual lives.

Partnering with Parents

Even with the most organized, creative, and Gospel-centered lessons, lives and hearts won't be changed if children aren't attending. That's why it's essential to build a bridge from the church to the home. Keep these things in mind as you work with parents of lower-elementary children:

Remember that you're on the same team. With spiritual development, avoid an "us vs. them" mentality. Yes, Scripture says the family is primarily responsible for faith training, but that doesn't let church staff and volunteers off the hook. We can work with parents and families of all kinds, intentionally supporting, equipping, and encouraging them. Send home practical follow-up ideas and discussion questions based on the weekly lessons. Keep in mind that not all children have a spiritual support system at home.

Be a reliable resource. Parents need practice being faith leaders. Inform them about family worship opportunities and other events that provide a safe place to share the Gospel with children. Point them toward classes and other parenting resources in your church and community. Stay current with issues and trends affecting families and kids, and be prepared to offer resources and Bible-based guidance for challenging situations.

Cheer on families. Christ-centered parenting is tough! Parents need to know we have their back—and so does God. Pray for families, and let them know you're doing so. Remind them that if they believe in Jesus, his Holy Spirit lives in them (see Romans 8:11) and works through them (Philippians 2:13). Many varieties of families exist these days, so make sure your language and communications reflect that.

Be in touch early and often. People usually need to see, hear, or read a message multiple times before it sinks in. So share information frequently, even if you feel like a broken record. Send emails or use a texting app to send parents follow-up information or details about an upcoming program or event. You also can communicate via blog, website, or social media (in a private Facebook group, for example). Share scheduling details, lesson themes, your vision, future plans, and more.

Harness parents' enthusiasm, but respect their time. Parents are great resources for ideas and publicity. Ask them to provide feedback on previous lessons and suggestions for future topics. Survey them to see which activities hit the mark and how much time they can reasonably devote to children's ministry activities in a typical week or month. Remember to ask parents for their prayer support, too. Even if moms and dads don't have time to assist in classrooms or chaperone activities, they may be willing to serve as prayer warriors on your behalf.

CHAPTER 10

UPPER-ELEMENTARY CHILDREN/PRETEENS
(FOURTH- TO SIXTH-GRADERS)

*T*he opportunity to offer spiritual guidance to older children and their parents is a special privilege. Long after your volunteer days are over, the preteens you've invested in will be proclaiming God's glory and telling other people about Jesus.

To minister to older children and influence them to follow Jesus for a lifetime, it's important to understand the world they're growing up in. Viewing that world from their perspective helps you make a greater impact on young lives.

In today's high-tech environment, children seem to grow up more quickly than ever. Before they're even teenagers, kids are exposed to content, challenges, and temptations that used to be off-limits until much later in life.

Referred to as "digital natives," older children don't know a world before the internet and smartphones. They typically spend several hours a day engaging with digital media, via multiple screens. They have no need for print materials, such as dictionaries or phone books, because everything's searchable online. From infancy, these kids have had entire networks catering to their entertainment around the clock. In this on-demand culture, kids have grown to expect instant gratification in all aspects of life.

Today's kids are busy with homework, sports, lessons, and outside activities. With all those packed calendars comes stress—for preteens as well as their parents.

These days, preteens are bombarded with messages of acceptance for all types of lifestyles and choices. Homosexuality and gender fluidity are now commonplace. In our "post-truth" culture, labeling anything as wrong or sinful is considered judgmental.

Violence and threats of violence also have become the status quo for children. Active-shooter drills are now part of the school routine. Kids born after the 9/11 attacks accept that gunfire and terrorism can break out anytime and anywhere—schools, churches, movie theaters, workplaces, and homes.

Characteristics of Preteens

Physically, upper-elementary children begin going through puberty. Girls typically enter that challenging stage before boys, sometimes as early as age 8 or 9. Preteens become very aware of how they look and may start spending more time in front of the mirror. Surging hormones can make young people more emotional or sensitive. As bodies change, kids may become clumsy and feel awkward and self-conscious. Because of this, preteens are prone to embarrassment; don't do anything in the classroom to accentuate those feelings.

Mentally, older children experience changing thought patterns. They're gradually able to think and reason abstractly. Because preteens are bombarded by information seemingly non-stop, they have short attention spans and are usually multitasking. Kids have learned to quickly scan for information that's relevant to them, and they expect answers to be available instantly, at their fingertips.

Socially, kids begin looking for advice and guidance from their peers. Friends become more important than parents (often to the dismay of moms and dads). Friendships are a big deal, because they give kids a sense of security. Preteens compare themselves to others and notice what their peers think and say about them. As a result, they spend lots of time, energy, and even money trying to cultivate a particular image and fit in with certain groups. Although interaction via screens is as natural for preteens as breathing, face-to-face communication may intimidate them. They'd rather text than talk, expressing emotion via emojis. Privacy is important to preteens, as well.

During this stage, as kids try to figure out their self-identity, they often feel insecure and inadequate. It means a lot to them when other people recognize and praise their accomplishments and character. Preteens are eager for someone at church to genuinely care for them and be a friend on their spiritual journey.

Testing the limits, a key trait of adolescence, begins emerging in preteens. They develop strong opinions and will argue with parents—and other adults—if allowed. Pushing the boundaries isn't a referendum on your teaching ability; kids are simply asserting themselves and their individuality.

Here are even more preteen traits—and how you can harness them in a learning environment:

- Preteens are willing to try new things. Surprise them!
- They enjoy exploring new ideas. Challenge them!
- They like hands-on, learning-by-doing activities. Engage them!
- They usually prefer to interact with members of their own gender. Group them that way!
- They seek role models in older people, specifically teenagers. Enlist youth to serve in your ministry!
- They want everything to be "fair." Avoid playing favorites!
- They desire more freedom yet still want adult help at times. Step back, but be available!

Teaching Tips

Knowing about common preteen traits boosts your effectiveness. Make the most of your time together with these guidelines:

Honor their attention span. If the average preteen attention span is about five minutes, you may wonder how you're supposed to keep it for an entire hour. The answer involves resetting kids' internal clocks every five minutes. Rather than viewing your time together as a 60-minute lesson, view it as 12 five-minute segments. For example, you can teach for about five minutes, have a group discussion for five minutes, teach again for five minutes, and then do a related activity or game. This type of pattern increases engagement and decreases discipline problems.

Let preteens talk...a lot. Allow plenty of opportunities for topical discussions. Yes, each class session should have some built-in quiet time for reflection and prayer. But for the most part, encourage kids to talk. Icebreakers are a fun way to get conversations flowing, especially at the start of a lesson. (See chapter 20 for ideas.) Throughout your meeting time, designate plenty of time for debriefing, asking questions, praying out loud, shouting out a memory verse, and more. In other words, your voice shouldn't be the only one that's heard.

Be a facilitator, not just a communicator. Lecturing is the least effective teaching method. People remember only about five percent of what you talk to them about. By contrast, the three most effective ways to retain material are (1) teaching others, (2) practicing by doing, and (3) having discussions. All three of those approaches put the adult leader in a position of facilitator rather than traditional teacher.

Explore tough questions with kids now. By high school and college, many young people who were raised in the church walk away from the faith. To help prevent that, be intentional about teaching kids why Christians believe what we believe. Dive into key tenets of the faith, such as why the Bible is true, and how we know Jesus rose from the dead. That way, when kids deal with doubts or have their faith challenged in high school or college, they'll have answers. You're teaching kids during a critical period and can set them on a path to follow Jesus for a lifetime. Encourage them to wrestle with their faith now, while they're with you and their parents, so they have a solid foundation to build on for the future.

> You're teaching kids during a critical period and can set them on a path to follow Jesus for a lifetime.

Teach strategically. With such a short window of time to help preteens form that firm foundation, you need a laser-focused teaching plan. Begin with the end in mind, and then take steps toward it. Sit down with your team to discuss this question: When kids outgrow our ministry, what do we want them to believe, embrace, and live out? The resulting answer should serve as the scope and sequence for your class. Use each lesson to guide preteens toward the truths they need to know and believe by the time they transition to youth ministry.

Here's an example of a one-year strategic teaching plan, with each topic representing a four-week series.

1. What it means to follow Jesus (salvation)
2. God made me (identity in Christ)
3. Worshiping God (worship and praise)
4. Relationship with Jesus (growing faith)
5. Following God's commands (obedience)
6. The Bible is true (apologetics)
7. God has a plan for me (purpose)
8. Loving others (relationships)
9. Living to give (stewardship and sharing)

10. Making wise choices (wisdom and discernment)
11. Sharing your faith (outreach)
12. Impacting the world (spiritual leadership)

Classroom Management

With preteens, expect occasional interruptions and off-topic questions. When disruptions continue and interfere with other students' learning, however, you'll need to put a stop to them.

For kids this age, two behavioral "strikes" should be sufficient, unless there are special circumstances. If a child causes a disturbance, remove him or her (or, ideally, ask an assistant to do so). In private, remind the child about the importance of listening when others are talking. Add that if misbehavior occurs again, the child will be removed for the rest of the time and parents will be notified. If that's necessary, talk to parents in private at pickup time.

For frequent behavioral issues, ask parents for ideas about how you can assist their child in cooperating. Something that's going on at home or school may be upsetting the child. Work with parents to help turn things around. You can even invite parents to attend class for a few weeks, if needed, to provide guidance.

Partnering with Parents

> If you want to truly influence preteens, you must begin by influencing their parents.

Don't wait until behavioral issues arise to get to know parents. They're the greatest influencer of preteens—for now. So, if you want to truly influence preteens, you must begin by influencing their parents. That requires shifting our focus toward helping parents follow God's plan for raising children in his ways and Word.

Remind parents to put God first. These days, parents feel pressure to set their kids up for success academically, socially, athletically, and financially. As mentioned earlier, that leads to packed schedules and increased stress. In children's ministry, you have the opportunity to encourage families to align their priorities with God's. Jesus instructs his followers—including families—to "seek first his kingdom and his righteousness, and all these things will be given to you as well" (Matthew 6:33). Always be thinking of ways you can connect with parents and encourage them to set priorities that honor God.

Keep in touch with parents. Maintaining regular communication is key, and "short and sweet" is fine. Texts almost always get read, so send brief messages to let parents know you're praying for them and their kids. Text a couple of questions from the lesson that they can discuss together at home. Connect with parents through social media too. Many probably use Facebook, so invite them to a private group where you post encouraging Scriptures, schedule updates, and photos from activities.

Assist with the transition to middle school. The move to junior high can be scary for parents as well as preteens. Walk alongside parents to make the transition go smoothly. Recommend books, resources, and websites (see chapter 19).

A few months before kids "graduate" from children's ministry, ask the youth pastor or director to visit your class. He or she can teach a lesson, make announcements, interact with kids, and describe various youth group activities. As the transition nears, involve the youth director even more to increase preteens' comfort with the move.

Finally, prepare preteens and parents for middle school by hosting a milestone event. Have families sit together and enjoy refreshments while you and some teammates recap ministry highlights and share words of encouragement. The youth director can offer advice about how to thrive during middle school. Have parents each write a note to their child, read it aloud to them, and pray for them. This is a special moment for kids, parents, and everyone who ministers to them.

CHAPTER 11

CHILDREN WITH SPECIAL NEEDS

It's 10:45 a.m., and the Sunday school hour is well underway. As worship music plays, some children jump enthusiastically near a stage while others stand by the door and just observe. Later, during the lesson, a teen assistant answers a child's questions and offers a fidget toy. Meanwhile, an adult volunteer beckons four children to a quieter corner of the room to create an art project. When it's time for small groups, two older kids hurry toward the lobby to join the adult usher team for the next church service. In a nearby classroom, two children look through a Bible storybook together inside a cardboard fort.

The casual observer might simply notice a gathering of happy children, busy and engaged in religious activities. But the success of this church's programming is due, in large part, to its special-needs initiatives. Because those are subtly woven into every aspect of the ministry, all the children in the example above can worship, learn, and serve.

> "We have seen *very special things* today."

An emphasis on welcoming people with disabilities to church isn't new; in fact, Jesus champions it during his earthly ministry! In Luke 5:17-26, people lower someone through the roof of a house. All they want is to get their friend, who's paralyzed, near Jesus. Although their method may have annoyed the homeowner, Jesus certainly isn't upset. Rather, the man is essential to Jesus' teaching that day. In fact, "All those who were there were surprised and gave thanks to God, saying, 'We have seen *very special things* today'" (Luke 5:26, NLV; emphasis added).

Today, of course, we don't need to pry open a roof to include families who are affected by disabilities. Churches can provide support in many ways. Some create tailored programs and hire specially trained staff. Others host outreach events and offer respite for caregivers. Some frequently adapt their ministry based on the specific needs of children currently in the congregation.

The particular programming method is less important than a church's overall culture. In 1 Corinthians 12, Paul presents a beautiful picture of the church as the body of Christ, reminding us that every part, every gift, and every person is indispensable. When a congregation grasps this important truth, an essential part of its mission involves including children with special needs.

With a "body-building" mindset as the foundation, children's ministry leaders then must build the programs and determine the procedures to make inclusion work well. For that, let's consider the purposeful, collaborative, and worshipful approach of the paralyzed man's friends.

Identify the goal. The Luke 5 innovators simply want to get their friend in the room with Jesus. Churches today have similar goals: provide access for children with special needs, offer support to their families, and help them participate in church life in comfortable and meaningful ways. Before launching programs or ordering curriculum, first establish your ministry's values and goals, which will serve as guideposts for decision-making and growth.

Assess any barriers. Our friends in Luke 5 take time to observe the barriers that exist for their friend. They notice the long line, observe the weather, and gauge the crowd's mood. They also know their friend and his needs. After gathering all this information, the group navigates around the barriers to make sure their friend isn't left out.

Common disabilities can create barriers to church participation. For example, loud music or crowded spaces may feel overwhelming to children with sensory-processing issues. Some kids may have difficulty reading fluently, while others struggle with fine motor skills. Attention disorders can make it tough to sit still, which may be interpreted as bad behavior but actually stems from a child's diagnosis. Taking time to understand these issues and anticipate children's needs builds a culture of respect.

> Taking time to understand these issues and anticipate children's needs builds a culture of respect.

While you're sizing up the challenges, also keep your eyes open for possibilities. Look at the church building, staffing availability, and every aspect of the ministry to identify ways you can welcome and care for all children.

Plan carefully. The Luke 5 crew develops a workable strategy to keep their friend safe and help him experience Jesus' teaching and love. The same principles apply in children's ministry: Focus on safety while finding accommodations that support learning and loving.

To begin, consider any necessary modifications to the environment. In addition to creating access for children with physical disabilities, consider staffing a sensory-friendly entrance away from loud music and crowds. With décor and lighting, aim for subtle colors and a less-is-more approach. Too much stimulation can lead to anxiety and distractibility.

Provide both structure *and* flexibility to enhance the ministry experience for children with special needs. Routines that make the program predictable can reduce anxiety and increase positive behavior. All kids do best when they know what to expect. Also offer options for less-structured activities, especially during worship time and group games, which can seem overwhelming to children with sensory issues. Offer alternative activities for kids who have difficulty remaining seated for a long time. They might benefit from a change of pace or an opportunity to serve elsewhere.

For curriculum, choose materials that are visually appealing and organized. This enhances readability for children with language-based learning disabilities. During discussions, add a few "yes/no" and "either/or" questions to the mix. Also remember to pause after asking a question. Some children might struggle with speech, but that doesn't mean they have nothing to say. Give kids time to formulate ideas. Make reading aloud and reciting verses from memory optional. Consider other ways for children to demonstrate their knowledge and faithfulness.

Difficulty with fine motor skills can affect children's ability to write or draw. Offer a variety of tools, such as markers and pencil grips, to make those tasks more manageable. Offer to scribe for kids who prefer that option. With crafts, anticipate children's needs by ordering extra supplies and offering support. Kids with motor planning issues may need additional attempts to create a craft.

Get creative with resources. Somehow, the Luke 5 team finds tools and rope to lower their friend through the roof. Likewise, we can identify resources and learning approaches that support kids with special needs and make them feel more comfortable.

Examples include:

- Illustrated schedules and other visuals to make the time predictable and understandable.
- Sensory tools, such as fidget toys and wiggle cushions, to manage anxiety or attention issues.
- Weighted vests or lap blankets to provide a sense of calm.
- A quiet room or sensory area (possibly in a pop-up tent or cardboard fort) where children can take a break.

> Identify resources and learning approaches that support kids with special needs and make them feel more comfortable.

- Dimmed lights and comfortable seating that creates an oasis of support.
- Hands-on tools, such as puppets or action figures, so children can retell stories and review concepts.
- Videos and software that allow kids to learn in different ways.

Work together. To realize its goal, the Luke 5 group relies heavily on teamwork—an approach that translates very well to children's ministry. Talk to the director about children's individual needs and how to meet them most effectively. Promote dignity by maintaining confidentiality, and set boundaries to prevent conversations from descending into gossip.

Collaborate with parents and assure them of your willingness to help. Some parents might be very forthcoming about their children's needs, while others may prefer to be more private. Build trust by sharing positive feedback with parents whenever possible. As relationships develop, parents may share important insights about how to best teach and relate to their children. Shared expectations and policies benefit kids as well as volunteers, staff, and parents.

Finally, remember that the folks in Luke 5 include the friend in their plans. He participates, too! Be sure to help children with special needs find ways they can serve the church and community. They're indispensable to your ministry and its mission.

Making accommodations and providing alternative activities doesn't dilute your lessons or their impact. Instead, it shows children and families that they're welcomed, loved, and needed—and that Jesus loves them, too. So take heart, and get ready to watch as God does very special things!

Special Needs Resources

Books

- *Autism and Your Church* by Barbara Newman
- *Every Child Welcome* by Katie Wetherbee and Jolene Philo
- *Children's Ministry Pocket Guide to Special Needs* (Group Publishing)
- *Mental Health and the Church* by Stephen Grcevich
- *We've Got This! Providing Respite for Families Affected By Disability* by Debbie Lillo

Ministry Organizations

- CLC Network — www.clcnetwork.org
- Joni and Friends — www.joniandfriends.org
- Key Ministry — www.keyministry.org
- Nathaniel's Hope — www.nathanielshope.org

Special Needs Websites

- Autism Speaks — www.autismspeaks.org
- Children and Adults with ADHD — www.chadd.org
- Learning Disabilities Online — www.ldonline.org
- National Alliance on Mental Illness — www.nami.org

SECTION 3

CHILDREN'S MINISTRY TOOLS

CHAPTER 12

CHILDREN'S MINISTRY
JOB DESCRIPTIONS

TEACHER

Teachers inspire children to learn about Jesus and participate in enrichment activities. They oversee an interactive classroom while demonstrating God's love for everyone. Teachers represent Jesus—and the church—to children and their parents.

Responsibilities

- Lead lessons and manage the classroom.
  - Prepare weekly lessons and activities ahead of time.
  - Arrive before class begins and remain until all children are picked up.
  - Take attendance (or make sure someone else takes it).
  - Present an engaging lesson, adapting to various learning styles.
  - Oversee crafts, games, songs, and other activities that reinforce the lesson.
  - Pray with children and other team members.

- Communicate with the children's ministry team and with parents.
  - Respond to emails and texts from the director and assistants. Inform the director if you'll be absent, giving as much notice as possible.

- ° Facilitate communication among the classroom team and the administrative helpers, as appropriate. Share schedules, ideas, and prayers for the weekly lesson.
- ° Interact with parents and other caregivers.

- Demonstrate a growing faith and love for God.
  - ° Attend worship regularly.
  - ° Pursue spiritual growth through Bible-reading, prayer, and fellowship with other Christians.
  - ° Reflect God's love by serving him and other people.
  - ° Reflect the fruit of the Spirit (see Galatians 5:22-23) while interacting with children, parents, and team members.

- Know expectations.
  - ° Understand the church's core values.
  - ° Know the ministry's policies and procedures.
  - ° Attend all training events.

Spiritual Gifts
- Teaching
- Leadership
- Service or hospitality

Supervisor: Children's ministry director

Relationships
- Report to the director. Be coachable and communicative. Consult with the director for direction or assistance, as needed.
- Oversee the assistant teacher(s), letting them know what to expect each week and what areas require the most help. Encourage and pray for the assistants.

Outcomes
- Children look forward to attending so they can learn about and experience God's love.
- The ministry team works together to guide children's spiritual development.
- The classroom is safe, secure, and nurturing.

Average Hours Per Week: About one or two hours during the week in preparation, communication, and prayer. About one-and-a-half hours on the day of the lesson.

Serving Period: One school year

ASSISTANT TEACHER

Assistant teachers help the lead teacher maintain a positive, interactive learning environment, pitching in as needed to keep things running smoothly. Assistants demonstrate the joy of service, lending a hand in a wide range of areas.

Responsibilities

- Support the lead teacher and help manage the classroom.
    - Read the lesson beforehand and come prepared to help.
    - Arrive before class begins and remain until all children are picked up.
    - Facilitate check-in and checkout, greeting children and parents.
    - Help take attendance, if needed.
    - Help children participate in all aspects of the lesson.
    - Help with crafts, games, songs, and other activities that reinforce the lesson.
    - Pray with children and other team members.

- Communicate with the children's ministry team and with parents.
    - Respond to emails and texts from the director and lead teacher.
    - Inform the lead teacher if you'll be absent from class, giving as much notice as possible.
    - Facilitate communication among the classroom team and administrative helpers, as appropriate. Share schedules, ideas, and prayers for the weekly lesson.
    - Interact with parents and other caregivers.

- Demonstrate a growing faith and love for God.
  - Attend worship regularly.
  - Pursue spiritual growth through Bible-reading, prayer, and fellowship with other Christians.
  - Reflect God's love by serving him and other people.
  - Reflect the fruit of the Spirit (see Galatians 5:22-23) while interacting with children, parents, and team members.

- Know expectations.
  - Understand the church's core values.
  - Know the ministry's policies and procedures.
  - Attend all training events.

Spiritual Gifts
- Service
- Helps
- Hospitality

Supervisors: Lead teacher, as well as the children's ministry director

Relationships
- Report to and take direction from the lead teacher. Review weekly communications from the lead teacher and pray for him or her.
- Consult with the children's ministry director for any additional direction or assistance.

Outcomes
- Children look forward to attending so they can learn about and experience God's love.
- The ministry team works together to guide children's spiritual development.
- The classroom environment runs smoothly.

Average Hours Per Week: About half an hour during the week in preparation, communication, and prayer. About an hour-and-a-half on the day of the lesson.

Serving Period: One school year

NURSERY VOLUNTEER

Nursery volunteers care for God's youngest children, nurturing them so they feel loved in a safe environment where they learn about Jesus.

Responsibilities

- Maintain a calm, safe learning environment in the nursery.
  - In age-appropriate ways, tell babies and toddlers about Jesus and his love.
  - Arrive ahead of time and remain until all babies and toddlers are picked up.
  - Ensure that parents follow check-in and checkout procedures.
  - Keep toys and equipment clean and safe.
  - Pray with and for children and the other team members.

- Communicate with the children's ministry team and with parents.
  - Inform the director if you'll be absent, giving as much notice as possible. Respond to emails and texts from the director.
  - Facilitate communication among the classroom team and administrative helpers. Share schedules, ideas, and prayers from the weekly lesson.
  - Interact with parents and other caregivers.

- Demonstrate a growing faith and love for God.
  - Attend worship regularly.
  - Pursue spiritual growth through Bible-reading, prayer, and fellowship with other Christians.

- ○ Reflect God's love by serving him and other people.
- ○ Reflect the fruit of the Spirit (see Galatians 5:22-23) while interacting with babies and toddlers, parents, and team members.

- Know expectations.
  - ○ Understand the church's core values.
  - ○ Know the ministry's policies and procedures, as well as special rules pertaining specifically to the nursery.
  - ○ Attend all training events.

Spiritual Gifts
- Hospitality
- Service

Supervisor: Children's ministry director (and nursery director, if applicable)

Relationships
- Report to the director, alerting him or her to any problems or concerns in a timely manner.
- As part of the nursery team, communicate with fellow volunteers. Encourage and pray for them.

Outcomes
- Babies and toddlers are eager to be in the nursery, learning about Jesus.
- The nursery team works together to care for young children.
- The nursery environment is nurturing, clean, and safe.

Average Hours Per Week: About one or two hours during the week in preparation, communication, and prayer. About an hour on the day of the lesson.

Serving Period: From six to twelve months

ADMINISTRATIVE VOLUNTEER

Administrative volunteers ensure that the entire children's ministry program runs effectively and efficiently. They assist with a wide variety of behind-the-scenes tasks, such as registration, check-in and checkout, attendance, security, marketing, office support, supplies, and event planning.

Responsibilities

- Take care of various administrative details.
  - Assist with communications among the children's ministry team and with parents.
  - Handle registration and maintain classroom rolls.
  - Order and organize curriculum and supplies.
  - Help with special events and programs.

- Demonstrate a growing faith and love for God.
  - Attend worship regularly.
  - Pursue spiritual growth through Bible-reading, prayer, and fellowship with other Christians.
  - Reflect God's love by serving him and other people.
  - Reflect the fruit of the Spirit (see Galatians 5:22-23) while interacting with children, parents, and team members.

- Know expectations.
  - Understand the church's core values.
  - Know the ministry's policies and procedures.
  - Attend all training events.

Spiritual Gifts

- Service
- Helps

- Administration and organization

Supervisor: Children's ministry director

Relationships
- Consult with the director to determine needs and schedules.
- Respond to the needs of teachers and assistant teachers.
- Welcome new children and parents to the ministry and assist current families as needed.

Outcomes
- The ministry team feels well-supported and is able to minister effectively.
- Programs run smoothly for all children and families.

Average Hours Per Week: Varies, as determined by the children's ministry director

Serving Period: Varies

CHAPTER 13

SUPPLY LISTS

Lesson Supplies
- Children's Bibles and Bible storybooks
- Curriculum lesson plan and handouts
- White board (or easel) and markers
- Writing utensils

Craft Supplies
- Chenille stems (pipe cleaners)
- Cotton balls
- Crayons, colored pencils, and markers (in containers so groups can share)
- Glue sticks
- Hole punch
- Paper (white, colored, and construction paper)
- Paper plates (to make crafts and to hold crafts)
- Pencils and pencil sharpeners
- Scissors (age-appropriate)
- Stapler
- Tape (clear and masking)
- Yarn

Safety Supplies
- Clipboard with class roster
- Easy-to-read poster detailing emergency procedures

- First-aid kit (latex-free bandages and gloves, individually wrapped alcohol wipes, "ouch" report sheets to communicate with parents)
- Flashlights (with extra batteries), and/or light sticks

Free-Time Supplies

- Blocks and building supplies
- Books
- Cars and trucks
- Dolls and doll clothes
- Games
- Modeling dough
- Pretend-play toys (food, tools, dress-up center)
- Puzzles with large pieces

Snack Supplies

- Allergy-free snacks such as crackers and fruit snacks
- Hand sanitizer in easy-to-dispense containers
- Napkins
- Plastic containers to hold snacks that aren't individually wrapped
- Small disposable cups
- Water pitchers

Nursery Supplies

- Baby toys such as balls, rattles, and washable books (cleaned after every use)
- Blankets (washed weekly)
- Changing table and diaper receptacle (plus a place to wash hands)
- Diapers (in all sizes), wipes, and latex-free gloves

- Portable crib (with large wheels for evacuation, if necessary)
- Rocking chair
- Spray bottle of toy sanitizer (clearly labeled)
- Swing

CHAPTER 14

LEARNING STYLES

*K*ids aren't one-size-fits-all, so lessons shouldn't be either. People learn in a variety of ways, and by mixing up your teaching style, you're more likely to involve more children. And when you can get more children more involved, the lessons and Bible truths are more likely to stick.

In general, experts point to four main learning styles, which you can remember using the acronym VARK:

- **Visual**—These learners need to see photos, charts, graphs, and other visual aids to help make connections between ideas.
- **Auditory**—These learners need to hear information, recite it back, and ask questions about it.
- **Reading/Writing**—Interacting with text is the preferred learning mode for these people. They enjoy taking notes and quizzes, as well as receiving handouts.
- **Kinesthetic**—Also known as hands-on or interactive learners, these people need to move around, try things out, do role-plays, and so on.

In the 1980s, developmental psychologist Howard Gardner developed the theory of Multiple Intelligences, which identifies at least eight types of "smarts."

- **Linguistic (word smart)**—These people excel at working and playing with sounds and words. They learn best by saying, hearing, and seeing words. They enjoy writing, reading, and listening.

- **Logical-Mathematical (numbers and reasoning smart)**—Exploring patterns, experimenting, and reasoning out problems are fulfilling for these people. They gravitate toward science kits, brain teasers, computers, and items they can collect and categorize.

- **Spatial (picture smart)**—Some people think in pictures, making them visual learners. Films, videos, maps, cameras, building supplies, and art supplies all contribute toward their learning.

- **Musical (music smart)**—These people like humming, singing, and playing instruments. They're sensitive to sounds around them, preferring music, rhythm, and melody. They tend to learn well when music plays in the background. They're usually good at memorizing and can sing what they're trying to learn.

- **Bodily-Kinesthetic (body smart)**—Using the senses helps these people learn. They enjoy anything physical, including touching, moving around, hands-on activities, role-playing, and creative movement.

- **Interpersonal (people smart)**—These individuals enjoy other people, have lots of friends, and learn by interacting with others. In general, they like to communicate and organize.

- **Intrapersonal (self-smart)**—Working alone is the ideal situation for these people. They tend to be self-motivated, with deep thoughts, ideas, and dreams.

- **Naturalist (nature smart)**—These people learn from being outside, in the natural world. They need to observe laws at work and enjoy being surrounded by plants and animals.

Psychologist Thomas Armstrong has written extensively about applying Gardner's theory in schools and classrooms. Much of the information in Armstrong's books *Multiple Intelligences in the Classroom* and *In Their Own Way* also applies to children's ministry teachers and volunteers.

CHAPTER 15

SAFETY AND SECURITY

*C*hurch employees and volunteers must set the standard for above-reproach personal interactions. Children of all ages need to be safe—physically and emotionally—while in our care. Security policies and procedures are essential for protecting kids *and* for safeguarding adults who work with them.

| Always err on the side of caution. |

Unless a church setting feels safe, attendees won't trust its people or its teachings. Every aspect of your ministry environment needs to be comforting and reassuring, for children as well as for parents. With safety issues, always err on the side of caution. Just one questionable incident can have a huge impact on someone's life—and on your ministry.

Policies

Every children's ministry program needs a handbook or policy manual that addresses important safety topics. During training, the director should review policies related to:

- Requirements to serve in the ministry
- Volunteer application and screening process
- Volunteer job descriptions
- Code of conduct
- Sick policy
- Substitute policy
- Bathroom and diaper-changing policy

- Check-in and checkout policy
- Contacting parents
- Classroom ratios
- Emergencies

Procedures

Policies are only as good as the detailed procedures that churches put in place and follow. Here are some examples of best-practice safety procedures for children's ministry:

- All volunteers must go through a screening process that includes a personal interview, a background check, and reference calls. (Don't be offended when a church runs a background check on you, even if you're a longtime member. These days, that's a standard procedure to safeguard children.)
- Before any room is opened, at least two adults must be present.
- Maintain safe volunteer-child ratios. Children should never be left alone with only one staff member or volunteer.
- Use a check-in and checkout system that includes name tags. When picking up a child, parents must present their matching name tag.
- Staff members and volunteers also should check in and wear name tags, so parents and children know who you are.
- Put children's name tags in a visible location. For younger children, name tags may work best on their back.
- Learn the names of children in your class.
- Keep the class roster and emergency cards nearby. (See the template at the end of the next chapter.)

- Never touch a child in an area that would be covered by a swimsuit, and don't let children touch you in those areas.
- Never kiss a child or encourage them to kiss you.
- If a child initiates a hug, it's okay to return it. Side hugs and "A-frame" hugs are generally appropriate.
- Don't let children sit on your lap. Ask them to sit next to you.
- When children need to go to the bathroom, don't send them alone. Two adults should accompany them, and children should do as much for themselves as they can.
- When changing diapers, always wear non-latex gloves.
- Use caution with snacks, always checking for food allergies. With young children especially, the safest thing is to have parents provide snacks. When severe allergies exist, ban all food from classrooms.
- Always know where the first-aid kit is. If parents supply an EpiPen, know when and how to use it.
- If you ever notice anything suspicious or concerning, talk to the director right away. In most states, children's ministry workers are "mandated reporters" for child abuse.

CHAPTER 16

IN CASE OF EMERGENCY

*P*reparedness pays off. Know the step-by-step procedures for various types of emergencies, which should be displayed in each classroom. It's also a good idea to practice these procedures with occasional drills. If first-aid training is available, take the classes or a refresher course.

In case of emergency, try not to panic—for children's sake as well as your own. It's hard to think clearly unless you're calm. Say a quick prayer, whether aloud with children or silently.

As a volunteer, you should always have quick access to the class roll, children's emergency cards, and a phone. Also make sure first-aid supplies, a flashlight, and a security vest are nearby. Keep your cell phone with you (and charged) at all times, and make sure the director's number is entered in it. During an emergency, immediately call the director. If in doubt, don't hesitate to call 911 first.

If a child gets injured, quickly assess the severity. For minor injuries, use the supplies in the first-aid kit, contacting the director, as needed. Comfort the child and use your best judgment about whether to contact parents. If a child vomits, help him or her clean up as much as possible, then contact the director or parents.

For more serious injuries, seek outside assistance immediately. Call 911 for any life- or limb-threatening incidents. Then contact the director and parents. Follow first-aid protocols to stop any bleeding, but don't move a child who may have suffered a broken bone or spinal injury. Have an assistant remove other children from the scene.

Be aware of all exits, as well as the best routes to get to them. If there's a fire, take all children to a designated area or as far from the building as is safely possible. Avoid the parking lot because of the dangers of moving cars and emergency vehicles.

If the emergency is weather-related, take all children to a designated safe area indoors, away from windows. Be familiar with procedures for the natural disasters most likely to strike your particular region (earthquake, tornado, flooding, etc.).

If the threat is from a person or intruder, try to lock the doors. Move children away from windows and doors. If possible, huddle together in closets or under tables. Gather all the children together, make sure everyone is accounted for, and indicate that they need to stay quiet. Pray calmly (either silently or in a whisper, if possible), asking God to protect you and to make his presence known to each child.

> Explain in age-appropriate language what's happening.

If you're on lockdown due to any type of threat, explain in age-appropriate language what's happening and what expectations are in place. For example, "We need to sit here quietly for a while because there's some yucky weather outside. We're safe together, but we just have to be patient." Then engage children in a calming activity. Depending on the situation, you can play games that don't involve much movement (such as I Spy), tell stories, or sing songs. If you need to remain silent, you can show children pictures on your phone or let them quietly play with any nearby action figures or other quiet toys.

Wait until you receive the "all clear" from authorities or your director before releasing any children to their parents. (Keep in mind that a stranger may be a legitimate parent or the person who caused the emergency.) Realize that parents will likely be stressed.

Remind them you must make sure all children have been accounted for. Ask any parents you recognize to assist you, if needed. Your reassuring voice and calm demeanor will be key. Be kind but maintain control.

EMERGENCY CONTACT CARD

Check with the children's ministry director to make sure each child in your class has an updated emergency contact card on file. Here's a sample to keep in your classroom or at the welcome center where new families register for Sunday school.

Child's name:_____ Child's birthdate:_____
Child's grade in school: _____

Mom's name: _____ Phone: _____
Dad's name: _____ Phone: _____

Who is authorized to pick up this child? (Please list in order of preference.)

    Name:_____ Phone: _____
    Name:_____ Phone: _____
    Name:_____ Phone: _____

Allergies or other concerns

_____
_____
_____
_____

Other children in the family

    Name:_____ Age: _____
    Name:_____ Age: _____
    Name:_____ Age: _____

CHAPTER 17

WHAT TO DO IF...

*T*hankfully, true emergencies are pretty rare in children's ministry. But an assortment of other situations might arise occasionally, and it's best to prepare for them ahead of time.

Below are some situations to ponder so you can serve most effectively and make good decisions. For training purposes, you can discuss these situations with your ministry teammates, or even conduct role-plays based on them to gauge your reactions and to discuss various options.

What if only one or two children show up? Seize that as an opportunity to invest in those kids. Give them extra attention or dive deeper into the lesson than you would've been able to otherwise. You also might be able to combine your class with another, but first check with that teacher and the director. Some children love smaller groups, while others prefer being with lots of kids. Try to discern what's best for the kids who attend.

What if more children show up than usual? This is actually a blessing! Don't panic or pick up the pace, which can add stress. Instead, pause to thank God and ask for his wisdom. Notify the director that you need help and more craft supplies. While those are on the way, engage children in a "get to know you" game or icebreaker. For example, have them sit in a circle and take turns saying their name and one other fact, such as their favorite color or superhero. For older kids, each new speaker can repeat other people's information before saying their own. (Have kids help one another, if needed.) When more children than expected show up, you might want to have them sit and work in groups during the lesson. This helps you keep track of everyone and allows volunteers to assist with groups.

What if I end up with extra time at the end of the lesson? Depending on the amount of time remaining, you can repeat some songs or games that were a hit with kids. Younger children may prefer "free play" until it's time for pickup. While they're building towers or playing house, you can reiterate key points of the lesson or of godly behavior. For example, say, "Great job sharing! That's how Jesus says we are to treat other people." Keep some extra activity sheets handy for children who prefer to color or do table work.

- For older children, keep a few Bible-based games or puzzles handy. Depending on the class size, you can form teams or have everyone work together.
- Here are a few fun, easy ideas to use in a pinch:
- Charades—Act out events or people from the lesson or from other Bible stories.
- Hangman—Guess key words from the lesson, Bible book names, etc.
- Would You Rather?—Provide a series of two options based on the lesson; for example, would you rather be Jonah or the big fish? Have children indicate their preference for each either-or option by moving to one side of the room or the other. If there's time for discussion, have them share the reason for their choice.
- Preschool and lower-elementary games such as Simon Says are great time-fillers, too. Try to add a

biblical twist; for example, instead of Duck, Duck, Goose play Jonah, Jonah, Whale.

What if parents want siblings to stay together? This is usually fine, especially if a family is new to the church. Check with the director, or have parents talk to him or her. It's usually better for the older child to go with the younger child. Help the siblings meet new friends their own age, and try to return them to their regular classrooms as soon as possible.

What if parents want their child moved to an older (or younger) classroom? For Sunday school, it's best to keep children with their same school grade. But consult the director and parents for special situations, such as when a child is accelerated or held back in school. With younger children, this isn't usually a big deal, but it becomes more difficult when kids are older. If parents are insistent, ask them to talk with the director.

What if a child gets hurt or sick? Follow your ministry's procedures for injuries and illness (see chapters 15 and 16). While the child is being tended to, have another volunteer take the rest of the children to another area to pray. For example, pray: "God, thank you for always being with us. Please take special care of (name) right now. Help (name) know you're with him/her. In Jesus' name, amen." Keep children occupied with an appropriate quiet activity. If the room needs to be cleaned up (after someone vomits, for example), take children to the hallway and get assistance.

What if a child has a meltdown? Sit with the child on his or her level and talk quietly (or ask an assistant to do so). Generally, the child doesn't want the attention of the whole class. Say, "It seems like you're having a rough day. Can I do anything to help?"

Listen to the child, if he or she will talk to you. Then offer comfort and a word of prayer. If the child doesn't want to talk, try engaging them in an activity such as coloring or reading a book with you. If the meltdown continues, contact the director or parents.

What if children start fighting? Quickly separate the children, and don't take sides. Assume there was a misunderstanding. If possible, let the children who were involved quietly work out the problem on their own. Use positive language, explaining how the Bible says we should treat one another. Afterward, keep children on opposite sides of a group or in separate small groups, if applicable.

What if a child is continually disruptive? Ask for help—from the director, parents, and also the child. Parents are most likely aware of the behavioral issues and may have some good suggestions. Try to "catch" the child doing something right, and offer warm words of encouragement. When a child is disruptive, provide some space to regain control, possibly letting them sit in a special place or hold a special toy or object. Don't discipline a child in front of the class. Instead, you have several options. You can ask an assistant to sit with and help the child. You can ask the child to help you with an activity, if appropriate. If your church has a buddy program, ask for a companion to accompany the child during class. These special mentors, whether youth or adults, can make a big difference for a child who just needs some extra help.

What if the whole class gets out of control? Pause and pray for wisdom. Use an attention-getter (such as a clapped rhythm or flicking lights) and then quickly transition to a new activity. Recognize children who follow directions and participate well. Announcing that it's snack time also works, if you say that snacks are available for anyone who's sitting at the table with clean hands.

What if a child goes missing? Don't panic! The child is probably somewhere predictable, either in the bathroom or getting a drink. Younger children may try to hide from you or sneak away to try to find their parents. Have an assistant quickly check the bathroom and drinking fountain, and if the child still hasn't turned up, contact the director. Provide as much information as possible (when you last saw the child, what he or she was wearing, and where the class has been, if you were outside the meeting room). The director can step in, access other resources, and search beyond the room. Stay with your class and continue the lesson, praying with children if they're upset.

What if someone I don't recognize appears at the door? Walk to the door and ask, "Can I help you with something?" Look them in the eyes, be friendly, and look for other people in the hallway. Assume the stranger is lost, but don't let him or her enter the room. Notice details about the person so you can be helpful later, if needed.

What if someone (a child, parent, teammate) seems distant, distracted, or worried? Ask if you can do anything to help or if they need to talk. You also can ask, "What's one thing I can pray for you this week?" Then jot down a reminder so you'll stop and pray specifically for that request. Be sure to follow up with the person the next time you see them.

In your role as a children's ministry volunteer, try to assume the best of everyone all the time. A grumpy child may not be feeling well or may be stressed about something at home or school. A harried parent may just have a lot on his or her mind—don't assume they're avoiding you. The children's ministry director and pastor are very grateful for your service, even when they don't have time to stop by and tell you.

What if I have a rough Sunday and feel like quitting?
Everyone has a bad day from time to time. If class doesn't go as well as you'd hoped, don't be too hard on yourself or the children. God is still at work, no matter how "successful" a lesson seems. Kids learn something important every time you meet, and surely you do too. Don't give up!

On the other hand, if you often leave the classroom feeling frustrated or exhausted, talk with the director. There's probably a better fit for you in a different part of the children's ministry or church. You'll know you're in the right place when you come away energized and excited.

CHAPTER 18

FAQS

Q: What if I don't feel qualified to teach or help?
A: That's okay! Maybe you've heard the saying "God doesn't call the qualified; he qualifies the called." Step up, step in, and see how God works in your life. People are willing to help you learn the ropes, and you'll discover unexpected blessings along the way. It's also okay to know your limits. If you don't like to sing in public, ask another volunteer to lead music time. Maybe you're more comfortable doing crafts and can swap duties with another teammate. Do what you excel at, and be open to learning new things along the way.

Q: Do I have to volunteer every week?
A: No, but the more regularly you serve, the better it is for children—and for you. Routine is important, especially for younger kids.

Q: What if I'm sick?
A: Call the director, giving as much notice as possible. Keep a list of substitutes handy, and use it to help find a replacement.

Q: What if a child shows up sick?
A: If the parents are still nearby, talk to them about the symptoms you're noticing. Reference the ministry's policy about illness, and contact the director, as needed, for backup.

Q: When I volunteer, can I bring a friend along?
A: Probably, but first check with the director. Any guest will need a background check and some training. Your friend may end up loving the ministry and joining you regularly.

Q: What if a lesson just doesn't click with me—or with children?
A: Adjust it! You can keep the same Bible lesson while changing up the delivery, game, or craft. If you think a different approach will work better with your class, try it. But if you're making a major adjustment or can't come up with alternative ideas, check with the director.

Q: What if I don't know the answer to a child's question?
A: That will happen sometimes, and it's fine. If you can't look up the answer in the Bible right then, tell the child you'll do some research. If it's a sticky question, encourage kids to talk with their parents about it. When children ask questions, it shows they're thinking about the lesson content and its implications.

Q: How do I handle questions about scary things or world events?
A: Remind children that God is always with them, no matter what. God is with people who are having difficulties, too. God doesn't cause these hard things, but he does take care of people who ask for help. Beyond that, encourage children to talk with their parents about how they're feeling.

Q: How can I get children's attention without shouting?
A: To regain control of the classroom, try whispering. Or use an attention-getting system such as a clapped rhythm, a hand motion, or a flick of the lights. Practice and review it with children at the

beginning of every class so they get used to it. When you use the attention-getter, kids are likely to respond faster, and you'll avoid frustration and wasted time.

Q: How can I get young children to cooperate, especially when it's time to stop playing?
A: Point out examples of the behavior you've requested. If you ask children to put toys away and come sit in a circle, praise someone who's doing that. Then count how many children are already seated where they should be. This is a positive way to encourage others join in.

CHAPTER 19

CHILDREN'S MINISTRY RESOURCES

Books

- *101 Sunday School Activities on a Tiny Budget* by Martha Maeda
- *Big Picture Bible Crafts* by Gail Schoonmaker
- *Caught in Between: Engage Your Preteens Before They Check Out* by Dan Scott
- *Children's Ministry on Purpose* by Steve Adams
- *The Expert Interviews: All About Family Ministry* by Keith Ferrin
- *Family Ministry Field Guide* by Timothy Paul Jones
- *Fidget Busters: 101 Quick Attention-Getters for Children's Ministry* by Jolene Roehlkepartain
- *Have a New Kid by Friday* by Kevin Leman
- *The Humongous Book of Games for Children's Ministry* by Group Publishing
- *The Spiritual Growth of Children* by John Trent and Kurt Bruner
- A study Bible
- *Team Up! The Family Ministry Playbook for Partnering With Parents* by Phil Bell

Curriculum

Most curriculum publishers provide children's ministry tips on their websites. A list of links to the biggest "kidmin" publishers is available here:

www.kidmintools.com/2014/06/30/the-huge-list-of-childrens-curriculum-providers/

Magazines

- *Children's Ministry Magazine* (www.childrensministry.com)
- *KidzMatter Magazine* (www.kidzmatter.com/magazine)

Websites

- www.biblegateway.com
- www.biblestudytools.com/library/
- www.cefonline.com (Child Evangelism Fellowship)
- https://churchleaders.com/category/children
- www.commonsensemedia.org (for reviews)
- www.fourfivesix.org (for preteen ministry)
- www.godlyplayfoundation.org
- https://ministry-to-children.com/
- www.orientaltrading.com (for game supplies, decorations, and gifts)
- www.pinterest.com (for last-minute craft ideas)
- www.preteenministry.net
- www.relevantchildrensministry.com
- https://wellequippedvolunteer.com

CHAPTER 20

ICEBREAKER QUESTIONS

$\mathcal{U}$se these discussion questions to help children open up and start talking to one another. The icebreakers work well at the beginning of a lesson, when new kids join your class, and when time remains before dismissal.

Encourage follow-up questions, and make sure everyone has a chance to speak. If the group is large, have kids form smaller groups, trios, or pairs. Feel free to add more ideas to these lists!

Icebreakers for Younger Children
- What's your favorite game (or book, or movie, or cartoon character), and why?
- What person in the Bible would you want to spend a day with? What would you want to do together?
- What's your favorite kind of animal that God made, and why?
- If you could have any job, what would it be?
- What's something you're really good at? How did you get good at it?
- So far, what's your favorite thing you've done at Sunday school? Why?
- If you had to pick just one food to eat for a week, what would it be?
- Who makes you laugh, and how? How do you make other people laugh?

- What's a favorite gift or surprise you've received?
- What three words would you use to describe Jesus? (Or how would you draw him?)

Icebreakers for Older Children

- At church or Sunday school, what's the most surprising thing you've discovered?
- If you had been one of Jesus' twelve disciples, what would you have wanted to ask him?
- If you could live in another time or place, which would you choose, and why?
- What trait is most important to you in a friend? In a future spouse?
- Who inspires you—or who do you look up to—and why?
- If money weren't an option, what would you most like to do or experience?
- What's your favorite childhood memory, and why?
- Would you rather have one or two really close friends or dozens of acquaintances?
- What's your favorite quality about yourself? What are you most eager to improve?
- How do you most want to be remembered, and why?

CHAPTER 21

SCRIPTURES ABOUT
JESUS AND CHILDREN

*J*n the New Testament, Jesus welcomes children, points to them as models of faith, and heals them. Here are some Bible passages to inspire and encourage you in your ministry role:

Matthew 15:21-28

Leaving that place, Jesus withdrew to the region of Tyre and Sidon. A Canaanite woman from that vicinity came to him, crying out, "Lord, Son of David, have mercy on me! My daughter is demon-possessed and suffering terribly." Jesus did not answer a word. So his disciples came to him and urged him, "Send her away, for she keeps crying out after us." He answered, "I was sent only to the lost sheep of Israel." The woman came and knelt before him. "Lord, help me!" she said. He replied, "It is not right to take the children's bread and toss it to the dogs." "Yes it is, Lord," she said. "Even the dogs eat the crumbs that fall from their master's table." Then Jesus said to her, "Woman, you have great faith! Your request is granted." And her daughter was healed at that moment.

Matthew 18:1-6, 10

At that time the disciples came to Jesus and asked, "Who, then, is the greatest in the kingdom of heaven?" He called a little child to him, and placed the child among them. And he said: "Truly I tell you, unless you change and become like little children, you will never enter the kingdom of heaven. Therefore, whoever takes the lowly position of this child is the greatest in the kingdom of heaven. And whoever welcomes one such child in my name welcomes me. "If anyone causes one of these little ones—those who believe in me—to stumble, it would be better for them to have a large millstone hung around their neck and to be drowned in the depths of the sea. ... "See that you do not despise one of these little ones. For I tell you that their angels in heaven always see the face of my Father in heaven."

Matthew 19:13-14

Then people brought little children to Jesus for him to place his hands on them and pray for them. But the disciples rebuked them. Jesus said, "Let the little children come to me, and do not hinder them, for the kingdom of heaven belongs to such as these."

Matthew 21:15-16

But when the chief priests and the teachers of the law saw the wonderful things he did and the children shouting in the temple courts, "Hosanna to the Son of David," they were indignant. "Do you hear what these children are saying?" they asked him. "Yes," replied Jesus, "have you never read, "'From the lips of children and infants you, Lord, have called forth your praise'?"

Mark 5:22-24, 35-42

Then one of the synagogue leaders, named Jairus, came, and when he saw Jesus, he fell at his feet. He pleaded earnestly with him, "My little daughter is dying. Please come and put your hands on her so that she will be healed and live." So

Jesus went with him. ... While Jesus was still speaking, some people came from the house of Jairus, the synagogue leader. "Your daughter is dead," they said. "Why bother the teacher anymore?" Overhearing what they said, Jesus told him, "Don't be afraid; just believe." He did not let anyone follow him except Peter, James and John the brother of James. When they came to the home of the synagogue leader, Jesus saw a commotion, with people crying and wailing loudly. He went in and said to them, "Why all this commotion and wailing? The child is not dead but asleep." But they laughed at him. After he put them all out, he took the child's father and mother and the disciples who were with him, and went in where the child was. He took her by the hand and said to her, *"Talitha koum!"* (which means "Little girl, I say to you, get up!"). Immediately the girl stood up and began to walk around (she was twelve years old).

Mark 9:35-37

Sitting down, Jesus called the Twelve and said, "Anyone who wants to be first must be the very last, and the servant of all." He took a little child whom he placed among them. Taking the child in his arms, he said to them, "Whoever welcomes one of these little children in my name welcomes me; and whoever welcomes me does not welcome me but the one who sent me."

Mark 10:13-16

People were bringing little children to Jesus for him to place his hands on them, but the disciples rebuked them. When Jesus saw this, he was indignant. He said to them, "Let the little children come to me, and do not hinder them, for the kingdom of God belongs to such as these. Truly I tell you, anyone who will not receive the kingdom of God like a little child will never enter it." And he took the children in his arms, placed his hands on them and blessed them.

Luke 9:46-48

An argument started among the disciples as to which of them would be the greatest. Jesus, knowing their thoughts, took a little child and had him stand beside him. Then he said to them, "Whoever welcomes this little child in my name welcomes me; and whoever welcomes me welcomes the one who sent me. For it is the one who is least among you all who is the greatest."

Luke 18:15-17

People were also bringing babies to Jesus for him to place his hands on them. When the disciples saw this, they rebuked them. But Jesus called the children to him and said, "Let the little children come to me, and do not hinder them, for the kingdom of God belongs to such as these. Truly I tell you, anyone who will not receive the kingdom of God like a little child will never enter it."

John 4:46-52

... there was a certain royal official whose son lay sick at Capernaum. When this man heard that Jesus had arrived in Galilee from Judea, he went to him and begged him to come and heal his son, who was close to death. "Unless you people see signs and wonders," Jesus told him, "you will never believe." The royal official said, "Sir, come down before my child dies." "Go," Jesus replied, "your son will live." The man took Jesus at his word and departed. While he was still on the way, his servants met him with the news that his boy was living. When he inquired as to the time when his son got better, they said to him, "Yesterday, at one in the afternoon, the fever left him."

CHAPTER 22

DISCUSSION QUESTIONS

*F*or a team training meeting about the material in this handbook, use the discussion questions below. Open with an icebreaker for introductions, and then work through the questions, encouraging everyone to share their thoughts and insights. End with prayer and words of thanks for people's service and commitment.

1. How has children's ministry affected your life, whether as a child, a parent, a grandparent, or a volunteer?

2. What excites you the most about volunteering in children's ministry? Explain.

3. What, if anything, intimidates or worries you about being involved with children's ministry?

4. In what areas do you think your gifts or talents can be put to the best use in our children's ministry?

5. From your perspective, what are the biggest perks and the biggest challenges of working with each of these four age groups: Babies and Toddlers, Preschoolers and Kindergartners, Lower-Elementary Children, and Upper-Elementary Children/ Preteens?

6. What aspects of your previous experiences (as a family member, employee, volunteer, etc.) might help you as you serve in children's ministry?

7. What ideas or questions do you have about partnering with parents? Do you think it's easier to interact with children or with their parents, and why?

8. How might our children's ministry become more inclusive for children and families with various special needs?

9. After reviewing this handbook, what ideas are you most eager to try and why?

10. When children leave your classroom each week, what do you want them to take home with them? When kids graduate from our program, what do we want them to have learned and discovered?

ABOUT THE CONTRIBUTORS

The Writers
Danielle Bell, who has more than 21 years of children's ministry experience, serves as minister to children at Dawson Memorial Baptist Church in Birmingham, Alabama. She trains and speaks at churches and national conferences, writes curriculum for Gospel Project Kids, and contributes to *Children's Ministry Magazine,* which named her a Top 20 leader in the field.

Heather Dunn has been involved with children's ministry since age 12. She has led children's ministry programs in churches of all sizes. She has written and edited for Group Publishing, Standard Publishing, NavPress, and Christianity Today.

Brooke Gibson loves ministering to preschoolers and their families through the local church, as well as encouraging other children's ministry leaders through speaking and writing. Since 2008, she has served as minister to preschoolers at her home church, Dawson Memorial Baptist Church in Birmingham, Alabama.

Dale Hudson has served in children's and family ministry for almost 30 years, helping to build some of the largest, fastest-growing children's ministries in the United States. Dale is the founder and president of Building Children's Ministry, which helps churches create strong leaders, ministries, and teams.

Kal Otis, who has 32 years of ministry experience, serves as a pastor of family ministries, overseeing programs from birth through high school. Her child-development background fuels her passion to equip volunteers and parents to make the most of spiritual teachable moments. Kal is an author, a national speaker, and a columnist for *Children's Ministry Magazine*.

Katie Wetherbee, an educational consultant in Ohio, is passionate about helping families, schools, and churches work together. She has written special-needs columns for *Children's Ministry Magazine*, as well as columns for *K! Magazine* and curriculum for Standard Publishing. Katie's book, *Every Child Welcome*, helps ministry leaders include families affected by disabilities.

The General Editor
Stephanie J. Martin has worked in Christian publishing for 27 years. She writes and edits magazine articles, newsletters, books, Bible studies, and curriculum, contributing at ChurchLeaders.com, Communication Resources, Group Publishing, and *Children's Ministry Magazine*. Stephanie volunteers in the children's ministry at her church in Colorado.

How Can a Prayer Ministry Transform Your Church?

Whether you are part of your church's prayer ministry, or thinking about starting or joining a prayer ministry team, the *Prayer Ministry Volunteer Handbook* is for you!

We are often very quick to say we will pray for someone when we hear they are going through tough times, but do we actually follow through with our promise to pray for them? How many times do we turn to prayer only in times of crisis, as a last resort, or simply to ask things of God?

We need to make prayer the first course of action, guiding all of our life decisions. We must challenge ourselves to move beyond the dinnertime and bedtime prayers and progress to a thoughtful conversation with Christ.

Join authors David and Kim Butts as they explore how a well-equipped church prayer ministry team can serve as a model and an encouragement to support the members of the congregation, and even the pastoral staff, in their prayer journeys. Discover how you can make your church a house of prayer for all believers.

VOLUNTEER HANDBOOK

HOSPITALITY MINISTRY

Equipping You To Serve

OUTREACH MINISTRY GUIDES

Greg Atkinson

Be Our Guest

Whether you are a volunteer in your church's guest services ministry, or thinking about serving alongside ushers, greeters, welcome desk hosts, and parking lot attendants at your church, the *Hospitality Ministry Volunteer Handbook* is for you!

How does a member of community see your church? When they hear your church's name, what is their initial reaction? We want any individual who steps foot onto our church campus to immediately feel Christ's love through our actions toward them—the question is, are we doing a good job at accomplishing that mission?

We might not think of customer service and church hospitality in the same vein, but this book shows how a service mentality can make life-changing first impressions on newcomers. It's filled with specific, practical strategies and tools to help the hospitality ministry team show the love of Christ to every visitor.

Join author Greg Atkinson as he helps identify ways your church can increase its hospitality to the community around you, and, ultimately, reach those people for the Kingdom of God.

Practical Outreach Ideas and Ministry Tools

Never has there been a greater need to share the good news of God's love with those in our communities. This compact handbook shows how individual Christians and ministry teams can share the gospel by reaching out to and serving others.

Featuring 121 outreach ideas, this book helps to equip ministry teams with practical tools to serve families, children, youth, seniors, first responders, the oppressed and under resourced, millennials, single parents, local schools and businesses and more!

Designed for ministry volunteers, the book is a compact handbook of outreach ministry helps, which in addition to the dozens of outreach ideas also include outreach Scriptures and prayers, ways to share your faith, team discussion questions and recommended outreach ministries and resources.

This helpful little book is a great resource for equipping outreach ministry volunteers to serve others and to share the good news!

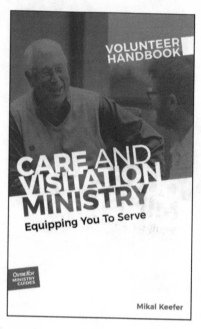

VOLUNTEER
HANDBOOK

CARE AND
VISITATION
MINISTRY
Equipping You To Serve

Outreach
Ministry
Guides

Mikal Keefer

Talk About More Than the Weather

You've driven to the hospital and stand outside a patient's room, ready to knock and ask permission to enter. But then what? How do you make a visit that actually matters?

Here are hundreds of practical tips gleaned from the experience of veteran visitors—chaplains, pastors, and volunteers who've made thousands of visits in hospitals, nursing care facilities, rehab centers, homes, hospice centers, even prisons.

They share what to do, what not to do, and how to connect in caring, compassionate ways with people who may be experiencing the worst days of their lives.

Discover how to make visits that matter—that literally change lives—as you carry the love of Jesus to those who are sick, lonely, or simply curious about the Kingdom.

Biblical Guidance and Practical Advice for Church Elders and Perspective Elders

Equip church elders to lead well. More than better methods, the church today needs better leaders. But too often we recruit these leaders (the New Testament calls them *elders*) without equipping them for their vital task. This practical handbook presents the need, lifts up the Bible's vision for elder ministry, and provides a wealth of practical how-to training to help elders provide the spiritual leadership that can't come from anyone else. Elder teams will build unity and confidence as they discuss it together.

Written by the ministry founders and leaders of e2: effective elders, content is based on decades of local-church experience and interaction with everyday elders in hundreds of congregations.

VOLUNTEER HANDBOOK

SMALL GROUP MINISTRY

Equipping You To Serve

OUTREACH MINISTRY GUIDES

Mikal Keefer

Equip Small Group Leaders to Lead Well

Your church's small group ministry is where faith can get real. Where masks can slide off and honest struggles and doubts surface.

Maybe. It all depends on the leaders of your groups.

Give your leaders the training they need to take group members deeper. To create group cultures that encourage transparency. To cope with questions, deal with doubts, and make disciples.

This book offers your team a lifetime of easy-to-read, easy-to-remember advice from experienced small group ministry leaders. They share what they've learned, what they wish they'd known earlier, and dozens of proven practical tips that will aid in developing healthy small groups in your church.